C000194484

CONTENTS

TECHNIQUES

PROJECTS

INTRODUCTION

I meet lots of dressmakers, both new and experienced, who are nervous of sewing with knitted fabrics, thanks in part to them often being found in the "difficult fabric" or "special fabric" sections of some sewing books. I think this reputation is unjustified as knits aren't as difficult to sew as you might have been led to believe; you just have to know the best way to handle them and no, an overlocker or serger is not essential. Certainly an overlocker can speed things along, but don't rush out and buy one just to sew knits—your domestic sewing machine can cope.

In this book, alongside projects for six core garments, I will give you all the background knowledge you need on knitted fabrics so that you can tell your jersey from your ponte roma, explain how to choose the right knitted fabric for your project, show you how to seam and hem knits using just your sewing machine, and then show you some special treatments for knitted fabrics. As well as all this, I'll share with you lots of tips that I've picked up during my twenty-six-year adventure of sewing with knits!

While working as a designer in the fashion industry, I spent four years at a loungewear company designing clothing specifically for wearing during yoga practice. The research I undertook while creating those garments, and the hands-on experience of working for a small company in which I not only did the design but also the pattern cutting and working directly with factories on production, left me with a love of working with knitted fabrics. It also felt like I'd come full circle as the first collection I ever produced as an eighteen-year-old student, was a knitted fabrics sportswear collection made entirely on my domestic sewing machine!

Whether you're new to sewing or a more experienced dressmaker who has developed "knit-phobia," you will be able to make a garment confidently with knitted fabric using this book. Many of my students sew with knits, often for their first ever dressmaking projects, and they all love the end results. After all, if you think of the clothes that you wear most often and that are the most comfortable, usually they're made from knitted fabrics.

I love sewing knitted fabrics and they always result in the most comfortable, wearable garments that usually become my go-to wardrobe favorites. I hope you'll soon feel that way too!

A BEGINNER'S GUIDE TO
SEWING
WITH
KNITTED
FABRICS

A BEGINNER'S GUIDE TO
SEWING
WITH
KNITTED
FABRICS

Everything you need to know to
make **20** essential garments

WENDY WARD

CICO BOOKS
LONDON NEW YORK

The measurements in this book are given in both imperial and metric. Please follow one system throughout and do not mix the two.

Published in 2018 by CICO Books
An imprint of Ryland Peters & Small Ltd
20–21 Jockey's Fields   341 E 116th St
London WC1R 4BW   New York, NY 10029

www.rylandpeters.com

10 9 8 7 6 5 4

A CIP catalog record for this book is available from the Library of Congress and the British Library.

ISBN: 978 1 78249 468 3

Printed in China

Editor: Katie Hardwicke
Designer: Geoff Borin
Photographer: Julian Ward
Illustrator: Wendy Ward
Stylist: Rob Merrett and Nel Haynes

In-house editor: Anna Galkina
Art director: Sally Powell
Production controller: David Hearn
Publishing manager: Penny Craig
Publisher: Cindy Richards

HOW TO USE THIS BOOK

• The easiest projects in the book, and the ones I recommend starting with if you're an absolute beginner dressmaker, are: Derwent Wide Leg Trousers; Longshaw Skirt; and Kinder Cardigan.

• For your first few projects using knitted fabrics, I recommend sticking to these fabrics: ponte roma, heavy single jersey, interlock, scuba, and lightweight loopback sweatshirt/French terry. These fabrics are easy to work with and will quickly build your confidence.

• In this book I show you how to sew knitted fabrics on your regular sewing machine without an overlocker (serger). However, if you do have an overlocker and enjoy using it then you can use it for all the seams, but you will still need to use your regular machine for hemming and topstitching. If you are lucky enough to own a coverstitch machine, you can use that for hems and topstitching.

• All six projects are for classic, basic garments that can easily be adapted to suit different styles and, together, can create a modern capsule wardrobe. The pieces are versatile enough in their style to be worn as everyday clothing, nightwear, or sportswear depending on your choice of fabric. For example, the Monsal Lounge Pants made in silk or viscose jersey would make gorgeous everyday pants, but made in soft cotton interlock or lightweight loopback sweatshirt, are the perfect pyjama pants.

• Fabric advice is given with each project, so refer to the What Fabric Should I Use? section in each project introduction. There is also a Glossary of Fibers & Fabrics on page 120 to help with fabric identification. It is important to pay close attention to the suggested spandex (elastane) content and stretch percentage when choosing your fabric. Detailed instructions are given in Know Your Knits, page 14, where you'll also find a quick guide to which fabrics suit which garments and a fabric shopping checklist to copy.

• Imperial and metric measurement systems are used throughout the book. Choose one system and stick with it throughout the making of a project.

• Read Sizing & Taking Measurements, page 12, thoroughly before starting any of the projects and take your measurements accurately.

• The techniques needed for each project are noted in the introduction to each project with page references, so read through these techniques before you start to sew.

• Full-size paper patterns for all of the projects are on pull-out pattern sheets inside the front and back cover of the book. Instructions for how to use them are given in Using Paper Patterns, page 23.

• Seam allowances are given at the start of the instructions for each project. All seam allowances are included in the patterns.

• Read through all the instructions carefully before you start to make sure you're following only the steps relevant to the version that you're making (each project has more than one version).

TECHNIQUES: TOOLS & EQUIPMENT

To sew knitted fabrics you don't need lots of specialist tools and equipment. A tool kit of good-quality dressmaking basics will cope with most jobs, alongside one or two bits of kit that will specifically help when working with knits.

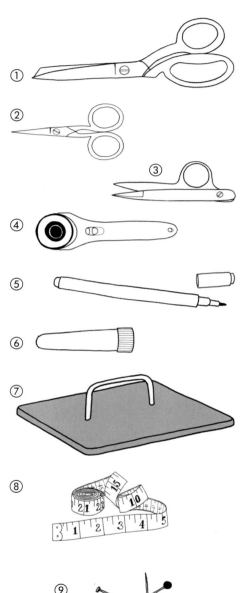

Tools for preparing and cutting your fabric

Scissors You will need at least three pairs:

① **Fabric scissors** Specialist fabric/dressmaking/tailor's scissors and shears have angled handles, which lets you keep the blades close to the cutting surface with the minimum lifting of your fabric. Long blades will speed up your cutting; blades at least 8 in. (20 cm) long are best. Never use fabric scissors to cut anything but fabric if you want them to stay nice and sharp. If they do start to get a bit blunt, ask your hairdresser where they get their scissors sharpened and take yours to the same place.

General-purpose scissors You need a separate pair of scissors for cutting out paper patterns. Again, a pair with angled handles and long blades make this job easier. An old pair of fabric scissors that have been used and abused can be relegated to this job.

② and ③ **Thread-cutting scissors or snips** A small pair of scissors with a very sharp point will be useful to keep by your sewing machine for cutting threads and for removing basting (tacking) stitches. Specialist thread snips are also useful for this job and are specially shaped to fit inside your hand, giving you maximum control over the cutting.

④ **Rotary cutter** Some people who sew a lot with lightweight, slippery knitted fabrics such as silk jersey, swear by their rotary cutters. To use a rotary cutter you will need to cover your cutting surface in cutting mats and it takes a lot of practice to be as precise with a rotary cutter as you can be with scissors. It's worth investing in two sizes: a bigger blade 1¾ in. (45 mm) for large simple shapes and a smaller one 1 in. (28 mm) for more intricate cutting.

Marking tools Knitted fabrics can be difficult to mark with traditional dressmaker's chalk and pencils, as they're too hard and simply drag and stretch the fabric. A marking pen or line can be used instead.

⑤ **Marking pen** Looks like a regular marker pen or felt tip, you can choose between temporary ink that simply vanishes over a few hours, or ink that is removed with water.

⑥ **Chaco liner** These work on most fabrics and are particularly good for knitted fabrics because they are filled with chalk dust, which means your marks can brush off easily, but you can get a very fine, accurate line.

⑦ **Weights** Use weights to hold your pattern pieces in place and get them nice and flat before pinning them onto your fabric. You don't have to use specialist ones, food cans or paperweights work just as well.

Pattern paper Specialist dressmaker's pattern paper is strong, but thin enough to trace through and often sold from a roll by the yard (meter) or in packs of pre-cut sheets. If you can't get hold of this, rolls of wallpaper lining paper or greaseproof paper used in baking are cheap alternatives, or even taped together sheets of newspaper.

⑧ **Tape measure** I prefer a plain and simple tape measure rather than the retractable ones that come in a little case, because they are cheaper and easier to use and store and the case on the retractable ones tends to get in my way.

Sewing tools

⑨ **Pins** I find there is a critical length with pins; too short and they're useless, too long and they just get in the way. My recommendation is no shorter than 1¼ in. (30 mm) and no longer than 1½ in. (35 mm), unless you're working with thick, bulky fabrics. You can get them with a bead head or without. I don't have a preference, but some find bead-headed pins easier to pick up.

⑩ **Magnetic pincushion** This is a gadget well worth investing in. No more dropped pins and you can virtually throw a handful of pins at it and they "stick."

Machine needles Most sewing machines come with a small pack of spare regular needles, but you will need to buy packs of ballpoint needles (or jersey needles) and stretch needles separately in order to sew many knitted fabrics. Regular and ballpoint needles are sized US 11/12/14/16 (UK 75/80/90/100): the lower the number, the finer (thinner) the needle. Stretch needles don't come in so many sizes. In general, thicker fabrics require thicker needles and vice versa.

There is a detailed explanation of how to choose the right needle for your fabric in Techniques—Setting up your Machine—Needles, page 21.

Hand sewing needles You need some hand sewing needles. Standard hand sewing needles are described as "sharps." They are sized differently to machine needles, with a higher number meaning a thinner needle for finer fabric. An assorted pack usually contains a selection of sizes from 5 to 10 and will be enough for most jobs when you start sewing.

⑪ **Needle threader** An inexpensive handy gadget. To use one, feed the small wire loop through the eye of the needle, place your thread through the wire loop and pull it back through the eye.

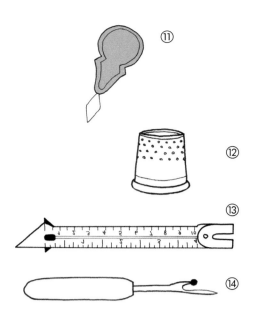

⑫ **Thimble** I must confess to being a recent convert to the humble thimble. After years of sore fingers I now use a tailor's thimble with an open top; it goes on your middle finger and you use the front of your finger to push the needle through the fabric. It takes some getting used to (there are some great videos online demonstrating the best technique), but your fingers will thank you! Thimbles come in different sizes and the right size is essential for good technique, so try on a few for size.

⑬ **Seam and hem gauge** This makes the job of marking seam and hemlines a lot quicker and easier. It looks like a short metal ruler with an adjustable guide that you can set to the measurement that you're working with.

⑭ **Unpicker** It is inevitable that, at some point, you will have to unpick something, even if it's just removing basting (tacking) stitches. Take care; unpickers are sharp and it's very easy to slip, resulting in holes in your fabric.

⑮ **Sewing machine** Probably the most expensive bit of kit you will buy, so it's a decision that requires a lot of thought and research. "Bargain" sewing machines on sale in supermarkets in my experience (and that of my students) aren't a good buy. Do your research, ask friends, look online, and, most importantly, go to a specialist sewing machine store and try a few. All you need, especially on your first machine, are:
• Straight stitch
• Zig-zag stitch
• A small selection of stretch stitches
• Buttonholes
• Ability to control the stitch length and stitch width
• A "free arm" (to slip sleeves and pant legs under the needle easily)

"Nice-to-haves" are:
• A speed control
• The ability to adjust the presser foot pressure.

Thread Which thread you use depends on what you are sewing:
• Basting (tacking): Use a bright color so that you can easily see to remove it, ideally something weak that you'll be able to break without too much effort, such as 100% cotton thread.
• Regular machine sewing: Use only branded sewing thread on your sewing machine. It is smooth and a consistent thickness—unlike cheap unbranded threads, which tend to be fluffy and slubby. Choose the polyester version as it is the strongest. Using cheap unbranded threads in your machine will lead to snapped threads, tangles in your machine, and tears.

Thread color Always unwind a bit of the thread and lay it on your fabric to choose the right color. If you can't find an exact match, go a shade darker; lighter colors tend to stand out and come to the foreground and so will be more obvious on your fabric. Darker shades recede into the background.

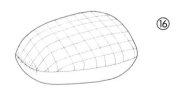

Pressing tools

Ironing board Get the biggest you can afford and have room for. Pressing is an essential part of dressmaking, and ideally you need your ironing board set up close to your sewing machine. Buying a separate reflective ironing board cover is also a worthwhile investment as it makes ironing quicker, won't get as dirty as a cloth cover, and adds an extra layer of padding to your board.

⑯ **Tailor's ham** So called thanks to its ham-like shape, a tailor's ham makes pressing curved seams and fiddly small areas so much easier. Once you have one you will use it almost every time you sew.

Pressing cloth A simple piece of unbleached cotton muslin is the cheapest and most used piece of pressing equipment in my workshop; when placed between your fabric and your iron it enables you to give your fabric a really good, long, hot press without the risk of scorching.

⑰ **Iron** Your iron should not be too lightweight; to press well, you need weight—so a lightweight iron actually means more effort is required from you! Make sure the sole plate has plenty of steam holes and has a nice long, tapered point at the end to make it easier to iron in and around those fiddly bits of your sewing. Also look for a variable steam setting, a long cable, and a large water tank.

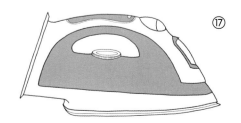

SIZING & TAKING MEASUREMENTS

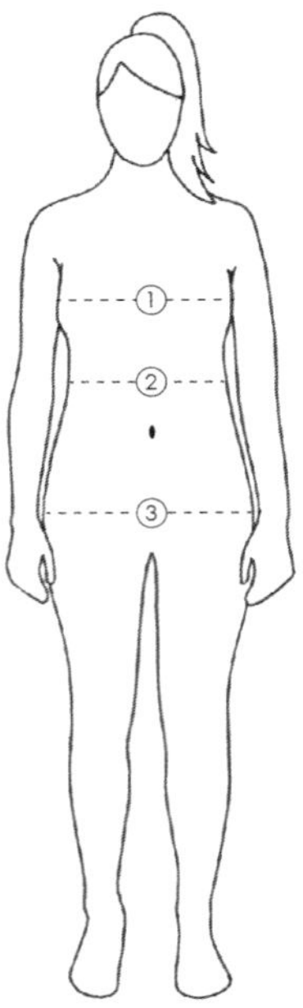

Sizing is a minefield because it can tap into many women's insecurities, but you have started on your journey into making clothes that fit your body, rather than trying to make your body fit into ready-to-wear clothes. When you don't sew, the only way that many of us keep a check on our body size is by trying on clothes in stores and looking at what the size label tells us. I'm guessing that in many of the stores you go into you're a different "size" in each one. It's a practice called "vanity sizing," where retailers give different "size" labels to the same set of body measurements according to what kind of customer they want to attract, which in my opinion makes dress sizes meaningless.

I want to be honest and totally transparent about sizing, that's why my patterns follow the system used in men's clothing and are based on actual body measurements. See How to Choose Which Size to Make, below, for details of the "sizes" used for the different projects based on hip, waist, or bust measurements.

Where and how to measure

To measure yourself you need to be standing, breathing normally (not sucking in your belly!), and the tape measure should be snug, but not tight (enough room to slide a couple of fingers underneath it). Don't measure loosely thinking that's how you'd like your garments to fit; we'll tackle that next, but for now you just need the actual dimensions of your body.

① **Bust** Measure around the biggest part of your bust; make sure that the tape measure is straight across your back, not sliding down, and have your upper arms down against your body when reading the measurement.

② **Waist** Tie something snugly around your middle, wriggle, and it will rest on your natural waistline. It is higher than you might have thought—just under your rib cage, well above your belly button. Measure your waist here.

③ **Hips** Measure around the widest part, which is usually the biggest part of your butt, right over your hip joint. Check the tape measure in a full-length mirror to make sure it is parallel to the floor. If your widest point is lower than this, make a note of that measurement, too, and choose your sizes based on this measurement.

How to choose which size to make

Here is my standard body measurement chart, which is the starting point for all the projects in this book:

	BODY MEASUREMENTS CHART									
	Size (actual hip measurement)									
Bust	31½ in. (80 cm)	33 in. (84 cm)	34¾ in. (88 cm)	36¼ in. (92 cm)	38 in. (96 cm)	39¾ in. (101 cm)	41¾ in. (106 cm)	43¾ in. (111 cm)	45¾ in. (116 cm)	47¾ in. (121 cm)
Waist	25¼ in. (64 cm)	26¾ in. (68 cm)	28¼ in. (72 cm)	30 in. (76 cm)	31½in. (80 cm)	33½ in. (85 cm)	35½ in. (90 cm)	37½ in. (95 cm)	39¼ in. (100 cm)	41½ in. (105 cm)
Hips	34¾ in. (88 cm)	36¼ in. (92 cm)	38 in. (96 cm)	39½ in. (100 cm)	41 in. (104 cm)	43 in. (109 cm)	45 in. (114 cm)	47 in. (119 cm)	49 in. (124 cm)	51 in. (129 cm)
	Based on a standard height of 5 ft 6 in. (170 cm)									

You probably won't match each measurement for a given size, because we are all different proportions.

The way the projects in this book are sized is dictated by what area of the body the garment will fit most closely. For each project, here are the measurements that you need to concentrate on matching most closely:

• Derwent Wide Leg Trousers
• Monsal Lounge Pants
These projects are sized on hip measurement with a size from 34¾–51 in. (88–129 cm), and these "sizes" are the hip measurements that they will fit.

• Kinder Cardigan • Peak T-Shirt • Winnats Tank
These projects are sized on bust measurement with a size from 31½–47¾ in. (80–121 cm) and these "sizes" are the bust measurements that they will fit.

• Longshaw Skirt
This project is sized on waist measurement with a size from 25¼–41½ in. (64–105 cm) and these "sizes" are the waist measurements that they will fit.

Some projects (Kinder Cardigan and Peak T-Shirt) have only 5 sizes, whereas all the others have 10. This is because the 5-size projects are fairly loose fitting and a single "size" can fit a broader range of measurements.

Taking ease into account

Your measurements and the body measurement size chart are a starting point, but next we need to consider the measurements of your garment once it's made. Each project in this book has a "Finished Garment Measurements" chart at the start of the instructions. These charts are the most crucial ones to check as they include ease.

Ease is the difference between your body measurements and the measurements of the finished garment. Unless a garment stretches to fit in places (like the Derwent Wide Leg Trousers and Winnats Tank), the finished garment measurements for a given size will always be bigger than those on the body measurements chart for that same size.

How much bigger depends on:
• The amount of wearing ease (the minimum extra added for the garment to be comfortable).
• The amount of design ease (the amount added to achieve the desired fit for the design ie. a fitted versus a baggy style).
By comparing the measurements from the two size charts, you will get an idea of how loose or fitted the garment is designed to be and how it's going to fit you.

Here are two examples for a size 41 in. (104 cm) hip:

Measurement	BODY MEASUREMENTS SIZE CHART Size 41 in. (104 cm) hip	FINISHED GARMENT MEASUREMENTS Size 41 in. (104 cm) hip	
		Derwent Wide Leg Trousers	Peak T-Shirt
Bust	38 in. (96 cm)		43¼ in. (110 cm)
Waist	31½ in. (80 cm)	30¾ in. (78 cm)	
Hips	41 in. (104 cm)	40¼ in. (102 cm)	43¼ in. (110 cm)

As you can see, the Peak T-Shirt is a loose fit on the bust and hips with 5½ in. (14 cm) ease on the bust and 2½ in. (6 cm) on the hips, as this garment is loose fitting all over.

Compare this to the Derwent Wide Leg Trousers, which is a snug fit on the waist and hips—the waist and hips are both ¾ in. (2 cm) smaller than the actual body measurements, as this garment stretches to fit the waist and hips. This is called NEGATIVE EASE and is where the garment is actually smaller than the body measurements, and it's only found in garments made from knitted fabrics that stretch to fit, hugging the body.

Adjusting the patterns

Garments made from knitted fabrics remove a lot of fitting problems. Part of their beauty is the comfort of the fit and very few fitting adjustments will be needed with the projects in this book because they are such simple classic shapes.

If you are in the middle between two sizes, I recommend going up and starting with the bigger size.

The only thing you may want to alter are lengths, and all of the projects have length options included on the patterns.

KNOW YOUR KNITS

What is a knitted fabric?

The main quality of a knitted fabric is that it stretches, much more than any woven fabric—even those with spandex (elastane).

The difference between a woven fabric and a knitted fabric is in their construction; woven fabrics have two lots of threads at right angles to each other, and if you look closely you will see some variation of a grid pattern formed by the threads going over and under each other. Knitted fabrics are made from interlocking loops and I often describe it to students as looking like hand knitting on a tiny scale. Detailed descriptions of all the fabrics referred to in this section can be found in the Glossary of Fibers & Fabrics, page 120.

Identifying the right and wrong side of knitted fabric

Correctly identifying the right or wrong side depends on the type of knitted fabric, as some knits can look almost identical on both sides of the fabric, but here are some clues to look for:

• Single jersey (typical T-shirt fabric) looks like hand-knitted stockinette (stocking) stitch and has tiny V-shaped stitches on the right side and tiny wavy stitches on the wrong side.

V-shaped stitches on right side

Wavy stitches on wrong side

• If your fabric has a knitted stripe (as opposed to a printed stripe), you'll be able to see a tiny line of both colours where the colour changes between stripes on the wrong side of the fabric.

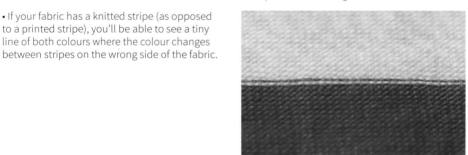

Knitted stripe from wrong side

• A print instantly gives the game away! Your fabric will be plain on the wrong side.

• In fabrics that initially look identical on both sides (such as interlock or ponte roma), see if one of the sides looks more uneven or rougher; that is usually the wrong side. The smooth, flat even color is on the outside of the garment.

• Some bouclé or boiled wools (sometimes called washed wool) may also look almost identical on both sides; usually they have a slightly more textured side and this is commonly used as the right side.

• Fabrics such as loopback or brushed back sweatshirt fabric/French terry, have a pile or textured side, which is usually used as the wrong side for warmth.

Loopback sweatshirt fabric with textured wrong side

• Single jersey has a tendency to roll along cut edges and selvages, which can also help you to identify the right and wrong sides. Almost always, cut edges along the width of single jersey will roll toward the right side and selvages will roll toward the wrong side.

Identifying the straight grain and selvages of a knitted fabric

Knitted fabrics still have a straight grain (grain line) that runs along the length of the fabric and it's even more important to get this right in knits than in wovens, as knitted fabrics tend to stretch most across the width: this is the part of your finished garment that will be wrapping around your body—exactly where you need most of the stretch!

The selvage (think "self edge") runs parallel to the grain line along the length of the fabric, so if your fabric has visible selvages, you've found the grain line.

To identify the grain line on knitted fabrics it depends on the type of knit, but here are some clues to look for:

• Sometimes you can see and feel blobs of glue along the selvages; lots of knitted fabrics are manufactured as a tube on circular knitting machines and this is where the tube has been cut. However, beware with cut circular knits, as the cut might not necessarily have been made perfectly straight along the grain line.

• On some knitted fabrics (single jersey, interlock, ponte roma, scuba, loopback sweatshirt/French terry) you can see the grain line. Look for the vertical lines in the rows of knitting running along the length of the fabric.

• Similar to identifying the right and wrong sides, the edges of single jersey fabrics have a tendency to roll and the selvages of single jerseys will roll toward the wrong side, so if you can find the edge rolling toward the wrong side, you've found the straight grain!

• Some knitted fabrics are "flat knitted" rather than being "circular knitted" and then cut. Ponte roma tends to be flat knitted and so will have very obvious selvages.

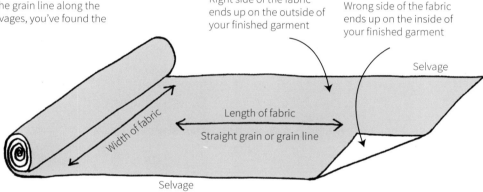

Right side of the fabric ends up on the outside of your finished garment

Wrong side of the fabric ends up on the inside of your finished garment

Selvage

Width of fabric

Length of fabric

Straight grain or grain line

Selvage

Vertical grain lines

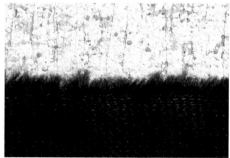

Selvage of single jersey runs parallel to these vertical lines formed by the stitches

Different types of knitted fabrics

Knitted fabrics can vary wildly and so it's good to be armed with some basic knowledge of the different types of knits, how they behave, and what they're best used for. I've divided them into two groups:

Full descriptions of the fibers and fabrics can be found in the glossary on page 120.

Light and medium-weight knits

Fabric names:
Single jersey
Interlock
Rib/ribbing

Common fibers used:
Cotton
Viscose
Silk
Wool
Spandex (elastane)

Best used for:
Tops and dresses in draped and fitted styles, lightweight drapey skirts and pants.
If you want to have a go at making sportswear, look for fabrics with an spandex content of 10%+, labeled as "4-way stretch" fabric.

Medium- and heavyweight knits

Fabric names:
Sweatshirt, Loopback (or brushed back) sweatshirt/French terry
Ponte roma
Scuba
Cut & sew knits (sometimes called "Sweater knits")
Boiled wool
Bouclé wool

Common fibers used:
Cotton
Viscose
Wool
Polyester
Spandex

Best used for:
As some of the fabrics in this group tend to have less stretch and are often referred to as "stable" knits, they're great for more structured/boxy styles such as loose fitting jumpers and dresses, loose fitting garments, and outerwear.

SUMMARY OF FABRICS AND FIBERS AND THEIR BEST USES:

Type of fabric	Best uses	Fiber content	Advantages & disadvatages
Lightweight delicate knits, eg. silk or viscose single jersey	Draped tops/dresses/skirts/nightwear/underwear	Silk	Cool, soft to wear, beautiful drape, lovely sheen
Lightweight T-shirt style knits, eg. cotton or wool blend jersey with or without spandex (elastane). Interlock Rib	Fitted styles/boxy shapes—will give a more structured effect to draped styles Nightwear, kids' clothes	Cotton	Cool, soft to wear, surface can look slightly fluffy or hairy, absorbent
		Viscose	Beautiful drape, creases easily and highly absorbent but slow to dry, which can make it uncomfortable to wear next to the skin
Medium-weight knits, eg. Loopback sweatshirt/French terry, ponte roma, scuba, cut & sew (sweater) knits.	Jumpers, boxy shapes, loose fitting dresses/outerwear/loose-fitting pants Scuba is great for very fitted body-con styles as well as looser more sculptured shapes	Polyester	Man-made fiber that isn't absorbent so can be uncomfortable to wear. Doesn't crease
		Wool	Warm and comfortable, but lightweight to wear, prone to shrinking, felting, and pilling
Heavyweight knits, eg. brushed back sweatshirt, boiled/felted wool, bouclé wool, cut & sew (sweater) knits.	Boxy, loose fitting styles, outerwear	Spandex (elastane)	Increases the amount a fabric stretches and dramatically improves a fabric's stretch recovery. Can also reduce the amount fabric creases

Working out stretch percentage

Each project gives a suggested stretch percentage as well as listing recommended fabrics. Stretch percentage is how much crosswise stretch a fabric has, ie. how much it will stretch across its width. This is important as not all knitted fabrics will stretch the same amount and some garments require a fabric to have more stretch than others, depending on how close-fitting the style.

For example, fabric with at least 50% stretch is recommended for the cuffs of the Monsal Lounge Pants to allow the fabric to stretch over the heel and still be a snug fit around the ankle.

To work out the stretch percentage of a fabric, cut a piece of the fabric that measures 4 in. (10 cm) along the width.

Holding each side of the fabric firmly, stretch it as much as you can alongside a ruler and make a note of the measurement it will reach.

Using this formula calculate the stretch percentage of your fabric:
Stretched length - original length = "A"
"A" ÷ original length x 100 = stretch percentage

For example, original length = 4 in. (10 cm), stretched length = 6 in. (15 cm)
6 – 4 in. = 2 in. ("A")/15 – 10 cm = 5 cm ("A")
2 ÷ 4 x 100 = 50% (5 ÷ 10 x 100 = 50%)

A fabric that stretches from 4 in. (10 cm) to 6 in. (15 cm) has a stretch percentage of 50%.

Stretch recovery

How quickly a fabric goes back to its original size or shape after stretching is called stretch recovery. A fabric that contains even just 3% spandex will have much better stretch recovery than fabric with no spandex content, and will keep its shape much better, meaning fitted styles won't "bag." For example, a fabric with some spandex content is recommended for the Monsal Lounge Pants to avoid baggy knees during wear, as the legs are quite a slim fit.

Fabric shopping checklist

Make some copies of this checklist to take with you when shopping for fabric for a new project. It will guide you on choosing the right fabric to suit the style of your pattern, tell you how much you should allow for shrinkage, and encourage you to keep all the relevant details of your potential fabric purchases, including the fiber content and washing instructions!

PROJECT:

Style:	Draped	Fitted	Boxy	Sculptural
	Viscose jersey	Cotton/elastane jersey	Loopback sweatshirt/ French terry	Ponte roma
	Silk jersey	Ponte roma with elastane	Ponte roma	Brushed back sweat
		Scuba	Scuba	Heavyweight cut & sew (sweater) knit
		Rib	Interlock	Boiled/felted wool
		Interlock	Cut & sew knit	
			Boiled/felted wool	
			Brushed back sweat (fleece back sweatshirt)	

Fabric requirements on pattern
yards or meters

Extra to buy to allow for shrinkage?
Cotton buy 10% extra / Viscose buy 8% extra / Wool buy 15% extra
yards or meters

Stick your fabric swatch here

Stick your fabric swatch here

Stick your fabric swatch here

Stick your fabric swatch here

SWATCH 1
Fiber:

Width:

Washing instructions:

Price:

SWATCH 2
Fiber:

Width:

Washing instructions:

Price:

SWATCH 3
Fiber:

Width:

Washing instructions:

Price:

SWATCH 4
Fiber:

Width:

Washing instructions:

Price:

PREPARING KNITS FOR A PROJECT

Pre-washing and shrinkage

Before you start cutting your knitted fabric you need to do some preparation. Always check the label when you buy your fabric to make a note of the recommended washing instructions (use the shopping checklist in Know Your Knits, opposite) and wash your fabric before cutting. If any fabric is likely to shrink it's a knit, especially cotton jersey and interlock. Here are a few things to remember when pre-washing your knitted fabrics:

• Viscose/rayon/bamboo can shrink by up to 8%, cotton can shrink up to 10%, and wool as much as 15%; allow for this when buying fabric as the fabric requirements in pattern instructions don't allow for shrinkage
• Shrinkage tends to occur most along the length of fabric
• Knits tend to shrink more than wovens as there's more movement in the structure of the fabric.

When pre-washing your fabric, ideally follow the recommended washing instructions, but in the absence of any instructions, put it on a cycle appropriate to the fabric and one that you'd like to be able to use on the finished garment.

As a very general rule of thumb, here is a guide to washing different fibers:
• Cotton can be washed on a regular cycle (105°F/40°C)
• Wool needs a cool (85°F/30°C or less) gentle wash with minimum agitation
• Viscose/rayon/bamboo should be washed on a cool (85°F/30°C or less) gentle wash
• Silk can be very gently machine washed at 65–80°F/20–30°C, or carefully handwashed with minimum agitation.

DRYING DO'S AND DON'TS

Knitted fabrics need careful handling when drying to avoid stretching and distortion. Here are some tips to help you keep your knitted fabrics in perfect condition:

DO

• Always dry knitted fabrics flat on a clothes airer.
• You can fold your fabric to fit on the airer, but make sure it's as flat and wrinkle-free as possible.
• Dry your fabric as soon as you've finished washing it to keep it crease and wrinkle free.

DON'T

• Drape knitted fabrics over any raised surfaces that will poke into the fabric and distort it, such as chair backs and banisters—the stretched and distorted areas that this will create in your fabric are extremely difficult to remove.
• Leave wet or damp fabric sitting in the washing machine or bowl, it will develop creases and wrinkles that will be almost impossible to remove.
• Never hang knitted fabrics on a line as the weight will make them stretch and they will stretch unevenly where you place the clothes pins.
• Tumble dry knits, especially those made from natural fibers and viscose/rayon/bamboo as it encourages shrinkage, pilling, and felting.
• Wring out silk, wool, or viscose/rayon/bamboo to remove water; instead gently roll in a towel and squeeze.
• Avoid direct sunlight when drying silk as it can damage the fiber.
• Silk can also be damaged by products containing alcholol, such as perfume.

Cutting

Read some of the tips in Know Your Knits, page 14, on how to find the grain line and how to identify the right and wrong side of your fabric before you start cutting.

Use pattern weights to hold your pattern and fabric flat while you pin or chalk around the pattern.

It is important to follow the relevant cutting plan for the version of the project you're making, ensuring you choose the correct one for your size and fabric width.

If your cutting plan requires you to fold your fabric, here's how to make a lengthwise fold in your fabric that precisely follows the grain line:

Finding the grain line

Don't assume that the selvages or cut ends of the fabric are straight, especially in fabrics that have been produced on circular knitting machines and then cut to create a flat open fabric with selvages—the cut can often be really off grain (ie. running at an angle to the grain line rather than along it).

Try to find the line of knit stitches in your fabric (this is easier on fabrics without a surface texture, such as single jersey, interlock, scuba, ponte roma, or the right side of loopback sweatshirt/ French terry). Once you've found it, this is the grain line along which to make your fold.

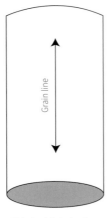

Tubular fabric that has been circular knitted

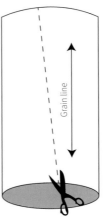

Tube is cut open to create open flat fabric with selvages

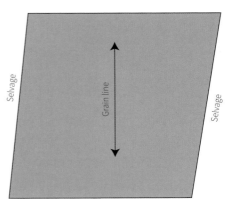

Slightly off-grain cut results in selvages that don't follow the grain line

Diagram 1

Selvages

Folded flat with square ends & no wrinkles

Fold along length of fabric

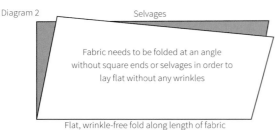

Diagram 2

Selvages

Fabric needs to be folded at an angle without square ends or selvages in order to lay flat without any wrinkles

Flat, wrinkle-free fold along length of fabric

You may find that your fabric, once folded, lies perfectly symmetrically (as in Diagram 1), but if you need to make what looks like an uneven fold to ensure the fold line is precisely on the grain line (as in Diagram 2) that's fine. The most important thing is to ensure that your fold is flat and wrinkle-free, any wrinkles along the fold mean that the fold is slightly off-grain.

If you cut your pattern off-grain (ie. with the grain line on your pattern not parallel to the grain line in your fabric), seams will twist.

TIPS FOR ACCURATE CUTTING

• If you are pinning your pattern onto your fabric, use a few more pins than you would normally and try to pin within the seam allowance.

• You might find it easier to pin your pattern to lighter weight knits while cutting out, but chalk around your pattern on heavier weight knits and remove the pattern before cutting.

• Lightweight knits with a tendency to roll will benefit from placing your pins at right angles to the edge of the pattern piece. For very delicate lightweight knits, consider investing in some fine ballpoint pins to avoid snags.

• When cutting your knitted fabrics, the most important thing is not to have your fabric hanging off the table or it will stretch—and once you've cut out your pattern pieces, they'll ping up shorter!

• If you can't fit all your fabric on the table, roll it up along the table edge.

• Don't snip notches on knitted fabrics, especially lighter weight more delicate knits, as a snip can easily run into the fabric and cause a ladder; instead, mark it with chalk or a fabric marker pen (see Tools & Equipment, page 10).

SETTING UP YOUR MACHINE & MACHINING TECHNIQUES

The one thing you absolutely must not do when sewing knitted fabrics on a regular sewing machine (unless your pattern instructions specifically instruct you to do so, when doing things like attaching neck bands and gathering) is stretch the fabric while sewing. If you do this, you will create a fabulously wavy seam or hem and it is impossible to correct this amount of stretching after sewing. Use exactly the same technique you would with a woven fabric; gently guiding the fabric through the machine, allowing the machine to feed the fabric through at its own pace.

Needles

The first thing you need to change on your machine when sewing knitted fabrics is the needle. There are two types of specialist needles available for sewing with knits on domestic sewing machines.

Ballpoint or jersey needles

Interchangeably called ballpoint or jersey needles, these specialized needles have a rounded point and so are more blunt than regular needles, enabling them to work through the gaps between the threads in the knitted structure of the fabric rather than piercing it, which avoids snags and ladders. Ballpoint needles come in different sizes, which correspond to the sizes of regular needles (see Tools & Equipment—Sewing Tools, page 10).

Stretch needles

These are very similar to ballpoint needles and also have a rounded blunt point, however, they are specially designed for very stretchy or bulky knitted fabrics and have a deep scarf (the groove above the eye), which helps the sewing machine to form a perfect stitch and so prevents skipped stitches. They tend to be available in fewer sizes, typically only US 11 (UK 75) and US 14 (UK 90). Twin needle versions of stretch needles are also available and they are the only twin needles I recommend for sewing twin-needled hem finishes on knitted fabrics (see Sewing Hems & Finishing Edges—Twin Needle Hems, page 28). Using a regular twin needle to hem knitted fabrics will cause lots of problems involving skipped, broken, and tangled stitches.

As with all sewing, save a scrap of your fabric from when you cut out your garment and do some test lines of sewing to get your machine set up correctly for that particular fabric.

Start by using the recommended needles in the chart. If you are encountering skipped stitches using a ballpoint needle change to a stretch needle. If the problems persist sometimes a regular needle can solve the problem on heavier fabrics.

GUIDE FOR WHICH NEEDLES AND SIZES BEST SUIT WHICH FABRIC:

Fabric	Needle Type	Needle Size	Tension
Light and medium-weight knits			
Delicate, lightweight single jersey, eg. silk, viscose, or bamboo jersey	Ballpoint	US 11/12 (UK 70/80)	3
T-shirt weight single jersey, eg. cotton jersey	Ballpoint	US 12/14 (UK 80/90)	4
Interlock	Ballpoint	US 14 (UK 90)	4
Rib/ribbing	Ballpoint	US 12/14 (UK 80/90)	4
4-way stretch (performance sportswear fabric): high spandex (elastane) content synthetic single jersey or interlock	Stretch	US 11 (UK 75)	4
Medium- and heavyweight knits			
Medium-weight loopback (or brushed back) sweatshirt/French terry	Start with ballpoint (if problems, use stretch)	US 14 (UK 90) US 11 (UK 75)	4
Heavyweight loopback (or brushed back) sweatshirt/French terry	Stretch	US 14 (UK 90)	5
Ponte roma	Stretch	US 11 or US 14 (UK 75 or UK 90), depending on fabric thickness	4
Scuba	Stretch	US 11 or US 14 (UK 75 or UK 90), depending on fabric thickness	4
Bulky and medium- to heavyweight Cut & sew (sweater) knits	Stretch	US 14 (UK 90)	5
Boiled wool/bouclé wool	Regular	US 14 (UK 90)	5

Tension

As with all fabrics, tension is important! Make sure the tension on your machine is set for the type of fabric and the type of sewing. If your machine has a numbered dial from 0–9, the following settings will be a good starting point for sewing seams in knitted fabrics:

Very lightweight knits (silk or viscose jersey): 3

T-shirt weight cotton jersey, ponte roma, scuba, interlock: 4

Heavier weight sweatshirting, and some cut & sew (sweater) knits: 5.

Presser foot pressure and the walking foot

Sometimes, despite your best efforts, your sewing machine might stretch your fabric, resulting in a wavy edge to your seam, especially when topstitching or hemming. If this happens there are two things you can do. The easiest, if your machine has the facility, is to reduce the presser foot pressure using a dial, usually found on the top of the machine. Reduce it by one setting.

If your machine doesn't have this facility, a walking foot can be really handy to prevent stretching; this has an additional feed dog on the underside of the foot that helps to feed the fabric through the machine more evenly. A walking foot tends not to come as a standard accessory and may need to be bought separately; buy the correct foot for your machine's make and model.

Common machining problems and solutions

• Always do a test seam on a reasonably sized piece of your fabric before you start on your garment, to ensure that you have all the settings correct for your fabric.

• Don't start sewing too near the edge of the fabric on lightweight knits—the machine will just "eat" your fabric, ie. it will get stuck in the hole in the needle plate. Start sewing approximately ⅜ in. (1 cm) in from the edge of the fabric.

• Don't reverse stitch at the ends of seams, especially on lightweight knits, as this encourages the fabric to disappear into the needle hole.

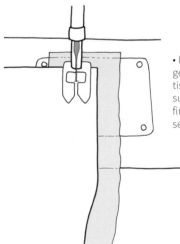

• If you're sewing a lightweight knitted fabric that keeps getting caught in the needle plate, place a sheet of tissue paper underneath your fabric while sewing. It will support your fabric and is easily torn away once you've finished sewing. This can also be used at the start of seams instead of starting away from the edge.

• Some lightweight single jerseys roll a lot along cut edges, making them awkward to sew; pin your seams with the pins inserted at 45 degrees to keep the rolling edge flat.

USING PAPER PATTERNS

Key to pattern pieces

The pattern pieces for all 20 versions of the six projects in this book are printed on the three pull-out pattern sheets included with this book, no enlarging or downloading required! You will need to trace off the pattern pieces you require, though, as the patterns overlap and the pattern sheets are printed on both sides. Follow the key on the pattern sheet as to which pattern pieces are on that layout, but here is a quick guide to where to find your pattern pieces:

Sheet 1—side 1:

1 Derwent Wide Leg Trousers—Front, part 1 of 2
2 Winnats Tank—Front
3 Monsal Lounge Pants—Front, part 2 of 2
4 Monsal Lounge Pants—Pocket band
5 Kinder Cardigan—Neckband, part 2 of 2
6 Kinder Cardigan—Short sleeve cuff

Sheet 1—side 2:

1 Derwent Wide Leg Trousers—Front, part 2 of 2
2 Winnats Tank—Neckband
3 Peak T-shirt—Back
4 Monsal Lounge Pants—Front, part 1 of 2
5 Kinder Cardigan—Back, part 1 of 2
6 Kinder Cardigan—Long sleeve cuff

Sheet 2—side 1:

1 Derwent Wide Leg Trousers—Back, part 1 of 2
2 Winnats Tank—Back
3 Monsal Lounge Pants—Waistband, part 1 of 2
4 Monsal Lounge Pants—Top pocket
5 Longshaw Skirt—Front & back skirt, part 1 of 2
6 Kinder Cardigan—Neckband, part 1 of 2

Sheet 2—side 2:

1 Derwent Wide Leg Trousers—Back, part 2 of 2
2 Peak T-shirt—Sleeve
3 Monsal Lounge Pants—Waistband, part 2 of 2
4 Longshaw Skirt—Front & back skirt, part 2 of 2
5 Kinder Cardigan—Back, part 2 of 2
6 Kinder Cardigan—Pocket

Sheet 3—side 1:

1 Winnats Tank—Armhole band
2 Peak T-shirt—Front
3 Monsal Lounge Pants—Back, part 1 of 2
4 Monsal Lounge Pants—Cuff
5 Longshaw Skirt—Waistband, part 1 of 2
6 Kinder Cardigan —Front, part 1 of 2

Sheet 3—side 2:

1 Peak T-shirt—Cuff
2 Peak T-shirt—Neckband
3 Monsal Lounge Pants—Back, part 2 of 2
4 Monsal Lounge Pants—Front facing & under pocket
5 Longshaw Skirt—Waistband, part 2 of 2
6 Kinder Cardigan—Front, part 2 of 2
7 Kinder Cardigan—Sleeve

Here is the best way to prepare your patterns

1 Check which pattern pieces you need to make your chosen project by reading the Preparing your Pattern Pieces section within the project instructions. This list also tells you if you will need to modify any of the pattern pieces to make your chosen version of the project.

2 Make sure you have read Sizing & Taking Measurements, page 12, and checked the finished garment measurement chart for the project you are making to choose the correct size.

3 Locate which pattern sheet the pieces you need are on and trace around the relevant pieces in your chosen size with a highlighter pen, so that you can see them clearly when tracing them off.

4 Carefully trace the highlighted pattern pieces onto dressmaker's pattern paper, large sheets of tracing paper, or greaseproof paper. Make sure your paper doesn't move while tracing: you need to be really accurate! If necessary, tape your sheets to a big table with masking tape or pin them together to stop them from moving away from each other.

5 As well as the shape of the pattern piece, also trace all the grain lines, darts, notches, and placement dots that appear within that pattern piece. (See page 24 for a full explanation of what all these symbols are for and why they are important.)

6 Some bigger pattern pieces have been printed in multiple parts, as they are too big to fit onto the pattern sheets in one piece. Where this is the case, you will see a broken "extension" line with scissors and numbered circles along the edge of the pattern where that piece ends (see above) and a corresponding extension line on the other parts of the pattern. Trace the first part of the pattern to the extension line, then align it with the extension line of the second part of the pattern (with the same numbered circles) to complete the pattern piece.

NOTE: All the patterns include seam and hem allowances. Seam allowances are usually ⅜ in. (1 cm), and hem allowances can vary but check the allowances given at the start of each project instructions.

Pattern markings

Make sure you transfer all the pattern makings when tracing your individual pattern pieces. All the pattern markings that you see are there for a reason and they will all help you to sew the garment together accurately. Here are explanations of what all the markings are for:

Grain lines These lines indicate where the grain line (or lengthwise direction of the fabric) should be when that pattern piece is cut out in fabric. Most of the time the grain line runs vertically through all the different parts of your garment once it is sewn together, but there are occasions when this isn't the case (see Know Your Knits, page 15, for a full explanation of the grain of the fabric). These marks don't need to be transferred onto your fabric; however, you do need to pay attention to them as they tell you how to position the pattern piece in relation to the straight grain in your fabric.

Place to fold line When the grain line turns in at each end at right angles, it means that the edge of the pattern that the arrows point to needs to be placed on a lengthwise fold in the fabric. You cut around all other sides of the pattern except this one on the fold and you will end up with one big symmetrical fabric piece once the pattern is cut out.

Notches Found on the edges of patterns on seam lines, these marks are used to help you match up seams accurately and to join the correct pieces together.

Placement dots For accurate positioning of things like pockets and sometimes used as an alternative to notches where there are lots of parts to match along a seam.

Transferring pattern markings

All notches and dots on your paper patterns need to be transferred accurately onto the wrong side of your fabric pieces once cut. Here's how to do it:

1 Keep your pattern pieces pinned to your fabric once you have finished cutting, then, using a fabric marking pen or chaco liner (see Tools & Equipment—Cutting, page 10), copy the pattern markings in the same position as they appear on the paper pattern, making sure you are accurate. You will need to lift up the edge of the paper pattern to mark notches with a single line on the edge of the fabric, but don't completely unpin the pattern as it will move around and you won't then be able to transfer the markings

accurately. To mark dots, unpin the pattern from the fabric in the area around the dot, place a pin through the center of the dot, and slightly lift the paper away from your fabric while leaving the pin inserted through all layers. You will then be able to accurately mark the position of the dot where the pin pierces the fabric.

2 If your pattern piece was cut out through two layers of fabric, you will need to transfer the pattern markings onto both pieces of fabric. Keep the pattern piece pinned onto the fabric and flip it all over so that you can mark the second layer of fabric on the back. Make sure you mark the wrong side of both layers of fabric.

Lengthening pattern pieces

Lengthening straight pattern pieces

Projects and pattern pieces that require modification:

• Derwent Wide Leg Trousers (standard and long leg versions)—trouser front and trouser back

• Peak T-Shirt (long T-shirt, short dress, and long dress versions)—T-shirt front and T-shirt back

• Kinder Cardigan (full-length version)—cardigan front, cardigan back, and neckband

1 Trace the relevant pattern piece to the length on the pull-out pattern sheet, leaving enough space at the hem/lower edge of the pattern to lengthen the piece.

2 Make a note of how much you need to add to the length of the pattern piece from the project instructions Preparing Your Pattern Pieces—Pattern Adjustments Needed.

3 Add this amount evenly along the hem/lower edge of the pattern piece and then extend the side seams and center front/center back lines to the new hemline.

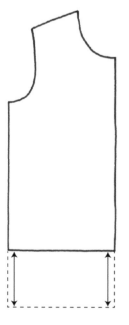

Lengthening shaped pattern pieces

Projects and pattern pieces that require modification:

• Winnats Tank (short and long dress versions)—tank front and tank back

• Longshaw Skirt (long skirt/ dress versions)—skirt body

1 Follow steps 1 and 2 for Lengthening Straight Pattern Pieces.

2 To keep the shaped side seams and hems, add the extra amount at regular intervals along the hem and then join up the marks. Extend the side seams and center front/center back lines to the new hemline, maintaining any flare along these lines.

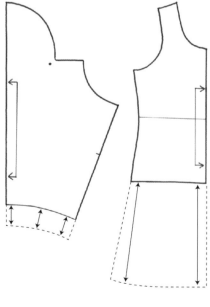

SEWING SEAMS

Make sure you have read Setting up your Machine, page 21, before you start to sew your fabric. I strongly recommend basting (tacking) all seams in knits to prevent stretching and to ensure your seams are accurate. Due to the stretchy nature of knitted fabrics, you can't sew them on a regular straight stitch; as soon as the fabric is stretched, the stitches would snap. You need to use a stretch stitch setting on your sewing machine. Here are three different ways to sew stretchy seams in knitted fabrics on any domestic sewing machine:

Stretch straight stitch

Zig-zag stitch used to neaten the edges of fabric

Stretch straight stitch (or lightning stitch!) Found on most modern sewing machines, this is the first and easiest stitch to use for seams in stretch knit fabrics and looks like a triple-stitched straight stitch or a narrow slanted zig-zag stitch resembling a bolt of lightning. Your sewing machine manual may describe it as anything from a triple straight stitch to a super-stretch stitch. This stitch is ideal for fabrics whose seam allowances won't unravel and don't need to be neatened, and for when you need to press the seam open to reduce bulk, such as in neck bands and cuffs. It's also a useful one for thick bulky fabrics.

• Edges can be zig-zagged to neaten but it's not necessary for ponte roma, most jerseys, or scuba as they won't shed; you may need to zig-zag on some loopback sweatshirt/French terry fabrics, which can shed a lot.

• If you do zig-zag seam allowances they're likely to stretch and look wavy—a quick press will flatten them down again, but for this reason seam allowances must only be zig-zagged AFTER the seam has been machined, otherwise the whole seam will be stretched out of shape.

Overlock stitch Another stitch found on most modern sewing machines. This stitch mimics the look of an overlocker (serger) stitch and can join the seam and neaten the edges in one go. The stitch on your particular sewing machine may look like any of the above; what you're looking for is a stitch that looks like a combination of a straight stitch and a zig-zag stitch.

The edge of the seam allowance can be trimmed off to neaten and the seam has to be pressed to one side, which means it isn't suitable for thicker fabrics. It works well on lightweight jerseys in cotton, silk, and viscose.

Stretch straight stitch seam allowances pressed open and left unneatened

Overlock stitch before seam is trimmed

Simple zig-zag stitch If you have an older or basic sewing machine it may not have any of the stretch stitches mentioned so far, but you can still sew knitted fabrics with a fairly short length, narrow zig-zag. This won't have as much stretch as the other stitches, but it will allow for some give in your seams. This seam can be pressed open or to one side.

QUICK GUIDE TO CHOOSING THE RIGHT SEAM FOR YOUR FABRIC AND PROJECT:

Type of fabric	Stitch to use
Light and medium-weight knits	
Delicate, lightweight single jersey, eg. silk, viscose, or bamboo jersey	Overlock stitch
T-shirt weight single jersey, eg. cotton jersey	Overlock stitch Stretch straight stitch for seams that need reduced bulk
Interlock	Overlock stitch Stretch straight stitch for seams that need reduced bulk
Rib/ribbing	Overlock stitch Stretch straight stitch for seams in neckbands, cuffs, and armhole bands
4-way stretch (performance sportswear fabric), high spandex (elastane) content synthetic single jersey or interlock	Overlock stitch or Stretch straight stitch if seam allowances don't unravel for seams that need reduced bulk
Medium- and heavyweight knits	
Medium-weight loopback (or brushed back) sweatshirt/French terry	Overlock stitch or Stretch straight stitch (with zig-zagged seam allowances if fabric sheds) for seams that need reduced bulk
Heavyweight loopback (or brushed back) sweatshirt/French terry	Overlock stitch or Stretch straight stitch (with zig-zagged seam allowances if fabric sheds) for seams that need reduced bulk
Ponte roma	Overlock stitch or Stretch straight stitch (with zig-zagged seam allowances if fabric sheds) for seams that need reduced bulk
Scuba	Overlock stitch or Stretch straight stitch to reduce bulk if seam allowances don't unravel
Bulky and medium- to heavyweight Cut & sew (sweater) knits	Stretch straight stitch (with zig-zagged seam allowances if fabric sheds)
Boiled wool/bouclé wool	Stretch straight stitch (with zig-zagged seam allowances if fabric sheds)

Accurate stripe matching

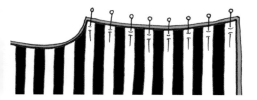 

Sewing stripes

1 Once you have cut out your pieces and you're ready to start joining seams, match up the stripes at each end of your seam and pin them accurately together. Then, work your way along the seam, pinning every stripe for wide stripes and every other stripe or every second stripe for narrower stripes. Place your pins at right angles to the edge of the fabric; you can fit in more pins and the pin is holding more of the stripe in place.

2 Open up a bit of the seam and double check that the stripes in between your pins are aligned.

3 Set your sewing machine to a basting (tacking) stitch (a straight stitch on the longest stitch length setting) and machine baste your seam together on the seam line—don't baste to one side because when you do your final stitching the stripes can move out of alignment.

4 Once basted, open the seam to check that the stripes are matching.

5 If they have moved, all is not lost. Your fabric is likely either to be very stretchy, a bit thick, or a bit "bouncy," and the top layer of your seam has been moved slightly by your machine, pushing the stripes out of alignment. Here's how to fix it:

• If your machine has the facility, reduce the presser foot pressure.

• Use a walking foot—the extra set of feed dogs on the walking foot will feed your two layers of fabric through the machine more evenly, without pushing the top layer and leaving your stripes out of alignment.

(See Setting Up Your Machine—Presser Foot Pressure and the Walking Foot, page 22, for more details on using both of these methods.)

(See Setting Up Your Machine—Presser Foot Pressure and the Walking Foot, page 22, for more details on using both of these methods.)

TIPS FOR CUTTING STRIPES

• Start with one prominent pattern piece (such as the front) and line up the same points on each pattern piece with the same part of the stripe. The easiest points to line up are the hemline or the top (underarm point) of the side seam.

• Always try and follow a stripe along straight hems.

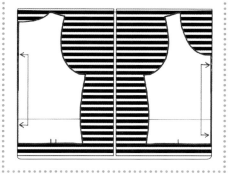

SEWING HEMS & FINISHING EDGES

Deciding how to finish the hems and edges of your knitted garment isn't as quick as just selecting a stitch and settings on your machine, as you do with seams. The shape of the hem or edge and where it is on your garment, as well as how much that hem or edge needs to stretch, will determine what technique you should use.

Hems

Preparing the hem

Hems in knitted fabrics require careful preparation to sew neatly. Always baste (tack) your hems in position before machining them—they can easily stretch out of shape and form tucks if you try to machine them pinned.

Start by turning up the hem by the required amount. Pin the hem in place (insert your pins at a 45-degree angle to help knitted fabrics that are rolling to lie flat) and baste close to the cut edge to hold it securely while you're machining. Use a contrast color thread that will act as a guide for where to sew, because most hem finishes in knitted fabrics look best if you machine them from the right side. When you have finished machining, remove the basting stitches and press the hem from the wrong side of the fabric to get a nice flat, crisp edge.

TIPS FOR SUCCESSFUL HEMS

• Always do a test on a reasonably sized scrap of your fabric before starting on the final hem.

• If the hem is stretching and going wavy when you machine the hem you can either: (1) Use iron-on stay tape (or a piece of lightweight fusible interfacing cut to the width of your hem allowance) along the hemline (not the cut edge of the fabric); (2) reduce the presser foot pressure; or (3) use a walking foot.

NOTE:

Method 1 is only suitable for hems that don't need to stretch as the stay tape or interfacing will stabilize the fabric and prevent it from stretching.

Three-step zig-zag hem

The first and easiest stitch to use for hems in stretch knit fabrics is also the stretchiest. Called a three-step zig-zag as the stitch is in the shape of a zig-zag, but made of tiny straight stitches. Most sewing machines have this stitch, it is sometimes called a "tricot" or "elastic" stitch as it's also used for sewing elastic onto fabric thanks to its ability to stretch a lot (see Special Treaments—Using Elastic to Gather, page 35).

This stitch is suitable for all hems, both straight and slightly curved, and will work on light and heavier weight fabrics. It looks neatest if you can manage to get the stitch sitting just over the cut edge of the hem on the wrong side of the fabric. Neat, accurate basting (tacking) will help. Practice first on a test piece of fabric.

Here's a guide to what settings to use on your machine:

• the widest stitch setting

• a slightly shorter stitch length than the middle setting (ie. if your stitch length goes up to 4, use 1.5 for this stitch).

Twin needle hem

Again, a technique that is easy to set up on most sewing machines. The machine is set for a normal straight stitch (with a slightly looser tension than you would normally choose for the fabric you're sewing) and you need to change the regular needle for a twin needle.

Twin needles are easy to get hold of and available in a range of sizes. Choose a stretch version in a size to match your fabric and a wide gap between the needles (at least ¼ in./5 mm). Attach the spare spindle to your sewing machine and thread it up with two needle threads (follow the instructions in your sewing machine manual for exact details on how to do this on your

particular machine). Using a regular tip twin needle rather than stretch can lead to tangles and skipped and broken stitches. (See Setting Up Your Machine & Machining Techniques—Needles, page 21).

This method is not suitable for all hems; use it for straight hems and those with a slight curve and light- to medium-weight fabrics. As this hem finish doesn't have much stretch, it isn't the right choice for hems that need to stretch a lot, such as hems on fitted pants or sleeves. Machine from the right side after basting (tacking) and try to position the left-hand needle close to the cut edge of the hem.

Simple zig-zag hem

If you don't have a three-step zig-zag or twin-needle facility on your sewing machine, a simple zig-zag works just as well. Use a wide stitch setting and a shorter than average stitch length as for the three-step zig-zag. Again, try and position your hem so that the stitch sits just over the cut edge of the hem on the wrong side of the fabric.

This stitch can be used in the same circumstances as the three-step zig-zag.

Edges

Folded band edging (T-shirt neck)

A finish suitable for very curved hems and edges, this is sometimes referred to as a T-shirt neck finish, but can be used on any curved edge including armholes (as in the Winnats Tank). A separate band of matching or contrast knitted fabric is attached to the edge of the garment so that it forms a visible edge—you can make a feature of it by using a contrast fabric.

The fabric used to make the neckband in the Peak T-shirt must have at least 35% stretch; 50% stretch is needed for the Winnats Tank as the edges are more curved and so the bands have to stretch more. See Know Your Knits—Working Out Stretch Percentage, page 17, for instructions on how to calculate this. If your main fabric doesn't have the required amount of stretch, use rib/ribbing in a matching or contrasting color; using your main fabric will result in an ugly edge that looks almost gathered and will never lie flat.

If you want to use this finish instead of a hem where there is no pattern piece, here is a guide for how to work out the size of your band (all dimensions include ⅜ in./1 cm seam allowances):

• Curved edges: cut the length of the band (running along the width of the fabric, ie. the stretchiest part of the fabric) approximately 4 in. (10 cm) shorter than the edge to which it will attach and 2–2½ in. (5–6 cm) wide (this makes a finished band ⅝–¾ in./1.5–2 cm wide).

• Straight edges: cut the length of the band to the actual measurement of the edge to which it will attach and twice the required depth plus ¾ in. (2 cm).

Making and attaching a folded band edging

This technique is great for very curved edges where you need to prevent the curved edge from stretching out of shape or where you want a more decorative edge. It's best for lighter weight knits due to the layers of fabric added by the band, but you could do this on a heavier fabric by using a lightweight jersey for the band.

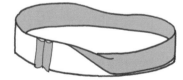

Neckband

1 Join the short ends together of your band with a ⅜ in. (1 cm) seam using a stretch straight stitch so that you can press the seam open. Press the neckband in half with wrong sides touching.

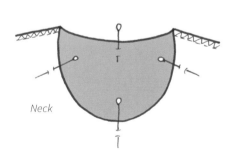

Neck

2 Divide the edge of the garment to which you're attaching the band into four:

• On necks, bring the shoulder seams together and mark center front (CF) and center back (CB) with pins, then bring those CF and CB pins together and, keeping the neck edges level, mark the four points with pins (remember, the four points aren't the shoulders as the front neck is longer than the back neck), the pins at the four marked points should be slightly forward of the shoulder seams.

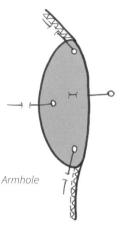

Armhole

• On armholes, bring the shoulder and side seams together and mark the four points along the front and back armholes.

3 Divide the band into four: fold it in half with the seam at one side and place a pin in the fold at the opposite side of the band to mark the halfway point. Refold with the seam and pin level and mark the two quarter way points with pins.

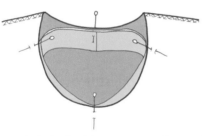
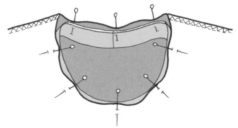

4 With the body of the garment inside out, pin the band to the right side of the opening at the four marked points—the single cut edge of the garment and the two cut edges of the band should be level. Position the seam in the neckband at the center back neck. Position the seam in the armhole band level with the side seam in the garment.

5 Once these four points are pinned (with pins at right angles to the cut edges of fabric), stretch the band between the four pins until the garment fits the band and add more pins. Gradually work your way around the band in this way.

6 Machine baste (tack) the band in place: the band should be uppermost when machining, and set your machine on a straight stitch on the longest stitch length to machine baste. This step allows you to easily fix the band in place without any tucks or wrinkles and to check that you've stretched the band evenly all around the opening. You'll have to stretch the garment slightly in between the pins while you're machining—pull the fabric gently in front of the presser foot while sewing, while allowing the fabric to be fed through the machine.

7 Turn through to the right side and check the band—a well-fitting band should sit flat with the folded edge lying flat against the body, not standing out away from the garment. Make sure there are no tucks in the seam and the seam is stretched evenly all the way round the opening.

8 Machine again with the band uppermost using your chosen seam type—the overlock stitch works well here as the seam doesn't need to be pressed open.

9 Press the band flat with the seam toward the garment and the band extending beyond the garment. A tailor's ham makes this easier.

10 Topstitch the seam toward the body. If the edge doesn't need to stretch when worn or when putting the garment on, you can use a regular straight stitch. If the edge does need to stretch (to get the garment on or during wear), use a stretch straight stitch (if your machine doesn't have this use a three-step zig-zag or regular zig-zag stitch). Stitch from the right side of the garment and give the seam a slight stretch while sewing if needed to keep it nice and flat to avoid any tucks or wrinkles.

11 Give the seam a final press to get a crisp, neat finish.

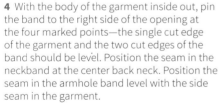

TIPS

• Ensure the shoulder seams remain pressed open or toward the T-shirt back (depending which stitch you used for the seam) while attaching the bands.

• Removing the free arm from your machine can help when sewing bands.

QUICK GUIDE TO CHOOSING THE RIGHT SEAM FOR YOUR FABRIC AND PROJECT

Type of fabric	Curved or straight edge	Does the edge need to stretch?	Hemming/edging method
Light and medium-weight knits			
Delicate, lightweight single jersey, eg. silk, viscose, or bamboo jersey	Curved	Yes	Three-step zig-zag or folded band
		No	Twin needle
	Straight	Yes	Three-step zig-zag or folded band
		No	Twin needle
T-shirt weight single jersey, eg. cotton jersey	Curved	Yes	Three-step zig-zag or folded band
		No	Twin needle
	Straight	Yes	Three-step zig-zag or folded band
		No	Twin needle
Interlock	Curved	Yes	Three-step zig-zag or folded band
		No	Twin needle
	Straight	Yes	Three-step zig-zag or folded band
		No	Twin needle
Rib/ribbing	Curved	Yes	Three-step zig-zag or folded band
		No	Twin needle
	Straight	Yes	Three-step zig-zag or folded band
		No	Twin needle
4-way stretch (performance sportswear fabric), high spandex (elastane) content synthetic single jersey or interlock	Curved	Yes	Three-step zig-zag or folded band
		No	Twin needle
	Straight	Yes	Three-step zig-zag or folded band
		No	Twin needle
Medium- and heavyweight knits			
Medium-weight loopback (or brushed back) sweatshirt/French terry	Curved	Yes	Three-step zig-zag or folded band in lighter weight fabric or ribbing
		No	Twin needle
	Straight	Yes	Three-step zig-zag or folded band
		No	Twin needle
Heavyweight loopback (or brushed back) sweatshirt/French terry)	Curved	Yes	Three-step zig-zag or folded band in lighter weight fabric or ribbing
		No	Twin needle
	Straight	Yes	Three-step zig-zag or folded band
		No	Twin needle
Ponte roma	Curved	Yes	Three-step zig-zag or folded band
		No	Twin needle
	Straight	Yes	Three-step zig-zag or folded band
		No	Twin needle
Scuba	Curved	Yes	Three-step zig-zag or folded band
		No	Twin needle
	Straight	Yes	Three-step zig-zag or folded band
		No	Twin needle
Bulky and medium to heavyweight Cut & sew (sweater) knits	Curved	Yes	Three-step zig-zag or folded band in lighter weight fabric or ribbing
		No	Twin needle
	Straight	Yes	Three-step zig-zag or folded bandlighter weight fabric or ribbing
		No	Twin needle
Boiled wool/bouclé wool	Curved	Yes	Three-step zig-zag or folded band in lighter weight fabric or ribbing
		No	Twin needle
	Straight	Yes	Three-step zig-zag or folded bandlighter weight fabric or ribbing
		No	Twin needle

SPECIAL TREATMENTS FOR KNITTED FABRICS

In this section, we'll look at some of the other finishes for knitted fabrics that differ to woven fabrics, including taping seams and different ways to use elastics.

Taping seams

In some knitted fabric garments you will not want particular seams to stretch. For example, I recommend using tape in the shoulders of the Peak T-Shirt and Kinder Cardigan when constructed in heavier or very stretchy fabrics, to prevent the weight of the garment dragging and stretching the neck and shoulders out of shape.

There are two ways of taping seams; either use plain cotton tape or iron-on bias tape (confusingly, it can also be known as: fusible tape, Vilene tape, bias tape, or fusible seam tape). I prefer iron-on bias tape as it's soft, doesn't add any bulk, and retains a bit of "give."

Applying iron-on bias tape

Iron it directly onto the wrong side of your cut garment pieces so that the tape covers the seam lines that you want to stabilize. Make your garment as normal and stitch on top of the tape when sewing that seam (just like regular interfacing).

Applying cotton tape

Lay the tape on top of the seam line before you join the seam, pin in place through all layers of the seam (including the tape), and machine all three layers in one go.

Using elastic as a waist facing

Using a deep elastic as a facing to finish the waist can achieve a smooth elastic waist finish without adding bulk, as used in the Derwent Wide Leg Trousers.

1 Once your circle of elastic and waist of your garment have both been divided into four (see Derwent Wide Leg Trouser instructions, page 65), you can attach the elastic to the waist.

2 With the garment inside out, place the elastic over the waist opening with the right side of the elastic touching the wrong side of the garment. Make sure the upper edge of the elastic is level with the cut edge of the waist of the garment and line up the pins with the four marked points in your elastic and your garment (line up the seam in the elastic with the center back seam in your garment).

3 Join the elastic to the waist edge of the garment using a zig-zag stitch. TIP: if you have an overcasting (also known as an overlock or overedge) foot, use this so that your zig-zag stitching encases the raw edge of the fabric.

> ### INTERFACING
>
> None of the projects in this book use interfacing, however there are occasions when it's a good idea to use some interfacing in your knitted fabric garment. Here are a few tips:
>
> • Which interfacing to use depends on what you're trying to do. To stabilize and strengthen part of a garment, such as a collar, cuff, or button stand made in knitted fabric, use a regular medium-weight iron-on interfacing to stop the fabric wrinkling and stretching.
>
> • To simply thicken and improve the drape and handle of the fabric, you can buy stretch fusible interfacing. It looks like a fine knitted fabric with glue on one side.
>
> • When using stretch interfacing it's crucial to make sure you apply it in the same direction as the stretch in your fabric—it stretches across the width but not the length (just like knitted fabrics).

4 Pin the loose edge of the elastic in place along the marked "facing fold line." Pin to the seams first, then in between to make sure that the elastic doesn't twist or form tucks (check on the right side once pinned in place). Machine in place with a stretch straight stitch close to the edge of the elastic.

5 Fold the elastic over to the inside of the garment (so that it's now sandwiched between two layers of fabric) and pin in place at the side seams and center seams. From the right side of the garment, machine a 1 in. (2.5 cm) long row of straight stitch in the center seams only to hold the elastic in place. Stitching from the right side of the garment ensures that your stitching disappears into the seam.

Elasticated waist—directly applied

To stop narrower elastic twisting and wrinkling in the waist of a knitted fabric garment you can attach the elastic directly to the waist edge rather than feeding it into a separate waistband, as used in this version of the Monsal Lounge Pants.

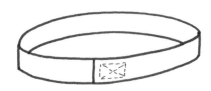
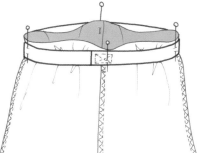
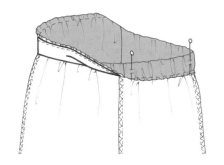

1 Overlap the ends of your cut length of elastic by ¾ in. (2 cm) to form a circle and securely stitch in place using a stretch straight stitch or zig-zag stitch.

2 Using pins as markers, divide the circle of elastic into four and do the same to the waist of your garment.

3 With the garment inside out, place the elastic over the waist opening with the elastic touching the wrong side of the garment. Make sure the upper edge of the elastic is just inside the cut edge of the waist of the garment, and line up the pins with the four marked points in your elastic and your garment.

4 Using a machine basting (tacking) stitch (longest stitch length, slightly looser tension), stitch close to the edge of the elastic and stretch the elastic to fit the garment as you sew.

5 Fold the elastic over to the inside of the garment so that it's sandwiched between two layers of fabric and pin in position, making sure that the elastic doesn't twist or form any tucks (check on the right side once pinned in place).

6 Stitch in place, again close to the tacked lower edge. Use a three-step zig-zag stitch and stretch the elastic again if needed on this second row of stitching so that the fabric can lie flat and not look twisted. The most important thing here is to ensure the fold in the fabric along the top of the elastic is snug against the elastic and that the elastic is stretched evenly so that the fabric lies flat when stitching.

Elasticated waist—in a waistband

This method involves feeding your elastic through a separate waistband applied to your garment; it is perfect if you're working with a bulky knitted fabric as you can use a lighter weight fabric for the waistband. This is also a nice way to introduce a contrast fabric to your garment, like in this version of the Monsal Lounge Pants.

1 Fold the waistband in half along the width with right sides touching, pin the short ends together. Machine, using a stretch straight stitch, making sure you leave a gap between the dots; you'll be threading your elastic through this gap in the seam later. Press the seam open.

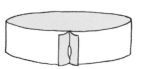

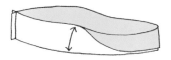

2 Fold the waistband in half along the length with wrong sides touching, aligning the two raw edges.

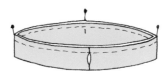

3 Press the fold to keep it in place, mark the center front and side seam notches with pins. Baste (tack) the raw edges together.

4 Divide the waist of the garment into four: bring the center front and center back seams together and mark the four points on either side with pins. For the Monsal Lounge Pants these points will be slightly back from the side seams, as the back of the pants is slightly wider than the front. For the Longshaw Skirt, you can use the side seams as the four marked points.

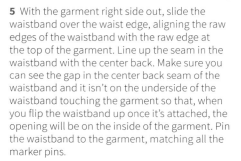

5 With the garment right side out, slide the waistband over the waist edge, aligning the raw edges of the waistband with the raw edge at the top of the garment. Line up the seam in the waistband with the center back. Make sure you can see the gap in the center back seam of the waistband and it isn't on the underside of the waistband touching the garment so that, when you flip the waistband up once it's attached, the opening will be on the inside of the garment. Pin the waistband to the garment, matching all the marker pins.

6 Baste and machine in place.

TIP

Be careful to keep this seam allowance really accurate or your elastic won't fit in the waistband.

7 Press the seam toward the garment and topstitch in place with a stretch straight stitch.

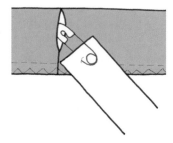

8 Once you have cut your elastic to length, attach one end to a safety pin and start to feed it through the gap in your waistband.

9 Keep pulling the elastic through the waistband, making sure the elastic doesn't twist and that the loose end doesn't disappear inside the waistband!

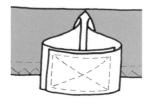

10 When you reach the beginning again, pull both ends of the elastic fully out of the waistband, overlap the ends by ¾ in. (2 cm), and pin in place. Using a regular straight stitch on your sewing machine, carefully sew the ends together. I tend to sew a square with a cross in the middle.

11 Let the elastic pull back into the waistband and close the gap in the waistband using a hand slipstitch.

Using elastic to gather

You can also use elastic to change the shape of garments. This method changes the Peak T-shirt Dress into a cute waisted style.

1 Join the ends of your cut length of waist elastic; overlap the ends by ¾ in. (2 cm) and secure with a line of short zig-zag stitches (this is the easiest stitch to use on narrow width elastic).

2 Using pins as markers, divide the circle of elastic into four.

3 With your garment inside out, fold it in half by lining up the side seams and use pins as markers along the marked elastic positioning line to mark the center front and center back, thus dividing the waist of the garment into four.

4 To attach elastic directly to the Peak T-shirt Dress: slide the circle of elastic over the dress so that the elastic is touching the wrong side of the dress and pin the elastic to the dress at the four marked points.

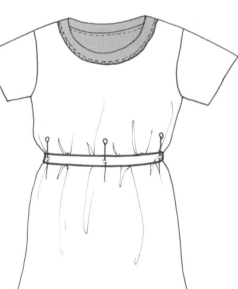

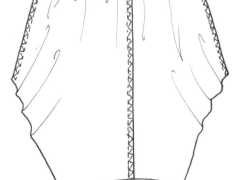

5 To attach elastic to the waist seam of the Longshaw Dress: have the dress inside out with the top of the dress down inside the skirt, place the circle of elastic over the waist seam of the dress, and pin the elastic in place at the four marked points.

6 Stretch the elastic to fit the garment between the pinned sections and insert more pins to hold the elastic in place.

7 Using a three-step zig-zag stitch (or a plain zig-zag stitch), stitch the elastic in place, stretching it to fit the garment in between the pins, removing the pins as you go. This stitching will be visible on the outside of the Peak T-shirt dress as the elastic is stitched directly onto the garment, but not visible on the outside of the Longshaw Dress as the elastic is attached to the seam allowance.

Elastic from right side of Peak T-shirt Dress

Elastic from wrong side of Peak T-shirt Dress

Elastic from right side of Longshaw Dress

Elastic from wrong side of Longshaw Dress

Shirring

This is a really easy technique for adding shape to a loose-fitting garment and a bit of textural detail.

1 Wind shirring elastic onto a bobbin from your machine. The elastic must be wound under a bit of tension, not stretched. You can wind it by hand onto a bobbin. To speed things up, use the bobbin winder on your machine, but hold the elastic in your hand so that it remains nice and loose on the bobbin.

2 Put the bobbin of shirring elastic into your machine and thread the needle with regular sewing thread.

3 Choose the settings for your machine: use straight stitch, with the length a bit longer than normal and the tension a bit higher than it should be set for the fabric.

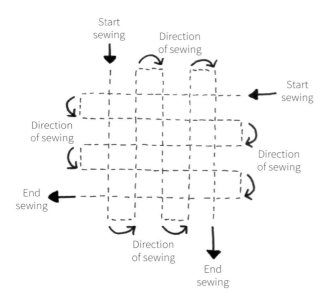

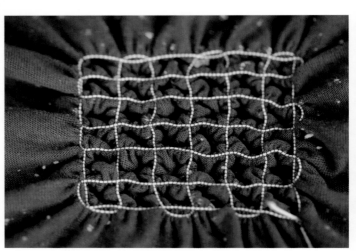

Shirring from wrong side

4 Stitch onto the right side of the T-shirt following the grid you have drawn in the direction of the arrows. Make sure you have long threads when you start to sew and don't reverse stitch.

5 After an inch or so of stitching you will see the fabric starting to gather up behind the presser foot!

6 When you come down the second row you will need to gently flatten out the bit of fabric that you're sewing. The fabric must be flat when you sew it, make sure that you're not accidentally sewing through another part of the T-shirt underneath.

7 When you come to the end of the first lot of rows, take the fabric out of the machine (again, don't reverse stitch) and leave long thread ends on the T-shirt and on the machine. Pull the top thread through to the wrong side of the T-shirt at each end of your line of stitching and secure the threads with a few knots. Don't cut the threads too short after knotting or they'll start to come undone!

8 Stitch the rows going in the other direction in the same way. You'll have to smooth the fabric out more to sew it flat this time.

9 Fasten off the ends of your sewing in the same way as before.

PRESSING

Press-as-you-go should be your only mantra when it comes to pressing. Your iron and ironing board are as important as your sewing machine when dressmaking—see Tools & Equipment, page 11, for advice on choosing and using pressing equipment.

Pressing is not ironing. Ironing is about removing creases; pressing is setting stitching, manipulating and controlling your fabric, and creating shape. Pressing also requires a different technique to ironing: when pressing, you need to apply varying amounts of pressure and heat in small areas, whereas ironing is maintaining a constant light pressure whilst moving the iron over large areas.

Try and get in the habit of pressing every seam once you have stitched it—"pressing as you go." Pressing seams not only makes any sewing that comes afterward neater (subsequent seams that cross this first one will match more accurately if your first seam is pressed nice and flat), it is also much easier in the long run.

Remember to check the washing and ironing instructions given with your fabric before you start, if in doubt (or if you don't have them), test your iron's temperature on a spare bit of fabric first.

Seams in knitted fabrics need to be pressed according to the type of stitch used—some can be pressed open, some need to be pressed to one side. Pressing instructions for each seam type are included in Sewing Seams, page 25. Always press hems to get beautifully crisp edges.

TIPS FOR PRESSING KNITTED FABRICS

• Always press on the wrong side of the fabric.

• Use a bit of steam to speed up and improve the finish of your pressing.

• Take care with prints; some may melt at higher temperatures.

• Man-made fiber fabrics need to be pressed at low temperatures, too high and the iron can leave a "shine" on the fabric or it can melt. Knitted fabrics particularly prone to this are scuba and ponte roma.

• Natural fiber fabrics can take higher temperatures, especially cotton, linen, and wool. The exception is silk, which must be pressed on a low temperature.

• Take care when pressing textured knits such as cut & sew (sweater) knits, boiled and bouclé wools—pressing too hot for too long can flatten the surface texture and the bulky/lofty quality of the fabric. Start on a low temperature with a pressing cloth and not too much pressure.

• Sequins or metallic prints can melt at higher temperatures.

• If you need to press the right side of the fabric, use a pressing cloth.

• When re-pressing areas with interfacing or iron-on stay tape, use a pressing cloth as the interfacing can still melt if caught with a too-hot iron.

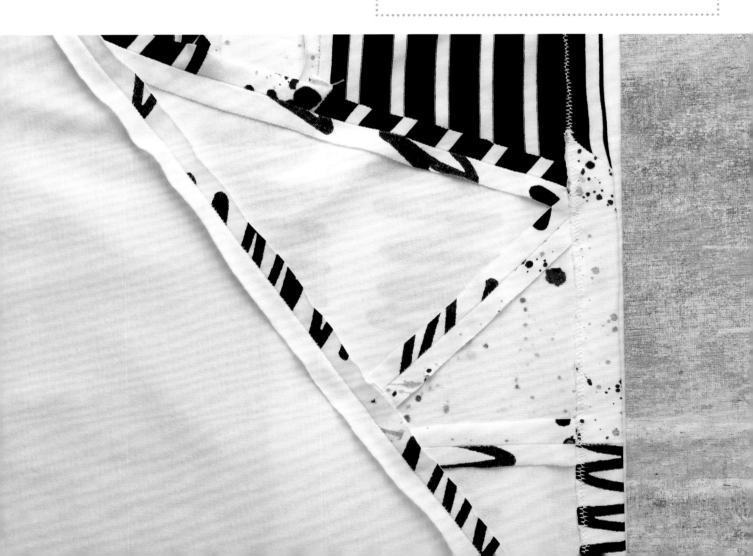

PEAK T-SHIRT

A basic crew neck T-shirt has got to be a staple in everyone's wardrobe. Not too tight, not too baggy, it's an endlessly versatile garment and an essential one to be able to sew yourself.

You can make this T-shirt long- or short-sleeved, with or without cuffs, hip skimming, bum covering, or as a T-shirt dress. Once you've mastered the basics with some plain versions, try using up some of your leftover fabrics on a patchwork corner, add some texture with a shirred detail, or mix and match fabrics with some color-blocked bands.

Make a batch of T-shirts in solid colors for your exercise class or have a go at honing your stripe matching skills and make a casual Breton-style T-shirt (which, by the way, looks great with the Derwent Wide Leg Trousers, page 58). Experiment with lengths and make a wardrobe of super comfortable and cool summer T-shirt dresses and mix it up a bit with some color blocking. A simple short-sleeved T-shirt dress with a shirred detail, teamed with some metallic sandals, will look amazing on your travels, and a plain white short-sleeved T-shirt will see you from the beach, to the gym, to lounging around the house on lazy weekends. Make a long-sleeved version with cuffs in a heavier weight fabric for the perfect sweatshirt.

If this is one of your first projects using knitted fabrics, choose a mid-weight cotton-rich single jersey—it will be the easiest single jersey to sew and get you off to a good start.

Follow the instructions in Sizing & Taking Measurements (page 12) for exactly where and how to measure yourself and how to choose which size to make.

WITH THIS T-SHIRT, YOU WILL PRACTICE THE FOLLOWING BASIC TECHNIQUES:

- Seams • Hems • Gathering
- Folded band edging
- Using elastic to gather
- Shirring

FINISHED T-SHIRT MEASUREMENTS

	Size (Your actual bust measurement)				
	31½–33 in. (80–84 cm)	34¾–36¼ in. (88–92 cm)	38–39¾ in. (96–101 cm)	41¾–43¾ in. (106–111 cm)	45¾–47¾ in. (116–121 cm)
Bust	36½ in. (93 cm)	39¾ in. (101 cm)	43¼ in. (110 cm)	47¼ in. (120 cm)	51 in. (130 cm)
Hem circumference	36½ in. (93 cm)	39¾ in. (101 cm)	43¼ in. (110 cm)	47¼ in. (120 cm)	51 in. (130 cm)
Back Length: Short T-shirt	22¾ in. (58 cm)	23½ in. (59.5 cm)	24 in. (61 cm)	24½ in. (62.5 cm)	25¼ in. (64 cm)
Back Length: Long T-shirt	26¾ in. (68 cm)	27¼ in. (69.5 cm)	28 in. (71 cm)	28½ in. (72.5 cm)	29 in. (74 cm)
Back Length: Dress	37¾ in. (96 cm)	38½ in. (97.5 cm)	39 in. (99 cm)	39½ in. (100.5 cm)	40 in. (102 cm)
Back Length: Long dress (not shown)	50¾ in. (129 cm)	51¼ in. (130.5 cm)	52 in. (132 cm)	52½ in. (133.5 cm)	53 in. (135 cm)
Sleeve Length: Short sleeve	7½ in. (19 cm)	7½ in. (19 cm)	7½ in. (19 cm)	7½ in. (19 cm)	7½ in. (19 cm)
Sleeve Length: Long sleeve	22 in. (56 cm)	22¾ in. (57.5cm)	23¼ in. (59 cm)	23¾ in. (60.5 cm)	24½ in. (62 cm)
Sleeve Length: With cuff	24 in. (61 cm)	24¾ in. (62.5 cm)	25 in. (64 cm)	25¾ in. (65.5 cm)	26¼ in. (67 cm)

WHAT FABRIC SHOULD I USE?

These T-shirts work in a wide range of knitted fabrics such as: single jersey, interlock, rib, loopback sweatshirt/French terry, brushed back sweatshirt/fleece, ponte roma, scuba.

Does my fabric need to have spandex (elastane)? No.

What percentage stretch does my fabric need? The fabric used for the T-shirt neckband needs to have at least 35% stretch.

If your main fabric doesn't have the required amount of stretch, use ribbing for the neckband (like my gray and green color-blocked version).

My samples are made in the following fabrics:

● Short-sleeved splatter print T-shirt: hand-painted 100% cotton single jersey

● Short-sleeved patchwork section T-shirt: main body 100% cotton single jersey; patchwork section stripe 97% viscose, 3% spandex single jersey, splatter print hand-painted 100% cotton single jersey, squiggle print hand-printed 97% cotton, 3% spandex single jersey

● Long-sleeved stripy T-shirt: 95% cotton, 5% spandex single jersey

● Short-sleeved shirred detail T-shirt: 48% cotton, 48% viscose, 4% polyester confetti effect single jersey

● Short-sleeved elasticated waist stripy dress: 100% cotton "rugby" jersey (heavier weight single jersey)

● Long-sleeved dress with contrast band: metallic gray 75% polyester, 21% Modal, 4% spandex, printed French terry/loopback sweatshirt; neon green 95% polyester, 5% spandex scuba and 95% cotton 5% spandex rib

If you are unsure whether a fabric is suitable, check the Glossary of Fibers & Fabrics (page 120).

YOU WILL NEED

For all versions

Matching sewing thread

For elasticated waist dress version

⅜-in. (1-cm) wide elastic—enough to fit around your waist

For shirred detail version

1 x reel of good-quality branded shirring elastic

FABRIC REQUIREMENTS

Size (Your actual bust measurement)

	31½–33 in. (80–84 cm)	34¾–36¼ in. (88–92 cm)	38–39¾ in. (96–101 cm)	41¾–43¾ in. (106–111 cm)	45¾–47¾ in. (116–121 cm)
Long T-shirt with long sleeves					
Fabric width 60 in. (150 cm) or wider	1⅔ yd (1.5 m)	1⅔ yd (1.5 m)	1⅔ yd (1.5 m)	1⅔ yd (1.5 m)	1⅔ yd (1.5 m)
Short T-shirt with short sleeves (plain or patchwork versions)					
60 in. (150 cm) or wider	1⅛ yd (1 m)	1⅛ yd (1 m)	1⅛ yd (1 m)	1⅛ yd (1 m)	1⅛ yd (1 m)
Long T-shirt with short sleeves (plain or shirred versions)					
60 in. (150 cm) or wider	1¼ yd (1.1 m)	1¼ yd (1.1 m)	1¼ yd (1.1 m)	1¼ yd (1.1 m)	1¼ yd (1.1 m)
Dress with short sleeves (plain or elasticated waist versions)					
60 in. (150 cm) or wider	1½ yd (1.4 m)	1½ yd (1.4 m)	1½ yd (1.4 m)	1½ yd (1.4 m)	1½ yd (1.4 m)
Dress with long sleeves (plain)					
60 in. (150 cm) or wider	1⅞ yd (1.75 m)	1⅞ yd (1.75 m)	1⅞ yd (1.75 m)	1⅞ yd (1.75 m)	1⅞ yd (1.75 m)
Dress with long sleeves (contrast band)					
Main fabric 60 in. (150 cm) or wider	1⅔ yd (1.5 m)	1⅔ yd (1.5 m)	1⅔ yd (1.5 m)	1⅔ yd (1.5 m)	1⅔ yd (1.5 m)
Contrast band 60 in. (150 cm) or wider	12 in. (30 cm)	12 in. (30 cm)	12 in. (30 cm)	12 in. (30 cm)	12 in. (30 cm)
Long dress with short sleeves (not shown)					
60 in. (150 cm) or wider	1⅞ yd (1.75 m)*	1⅞ yd (1.75 m)*	1⅞ yd (1.75 m)*	1⅞ yd (1.75 m)*	1⅞ yd (1.75 m)*

* add an extra 16 in. (40 cm) for a long dress with long sleeves

WHICH CUTTING PLAN TO FOLLOW

Size (Your actual bust measurement)

	31½–33 in. (80–84 cm)	34¾–36¼ in. (88–92 cm)	38–39¾ in. (96–101 cm)	41¾–43¾ in. (106–111 cm)	45¾–47¾ in. (116–121 cm)
Long-sleeved dress with contrast band	1a, 1b & 2	1a, 1b & 2	1a, 1b & 2	1a, 1b & 2	1a, 1b & 2
All other versions	1a & 1b	1a & 1b	1a & 1b	1a & 1b	1a & 1b

CUTTING YOUR FABRIC

Make sure you read the Preparing Knits for a Project section (page 19) and Using Paper Patterns (page 23) before you lay out your pattern pieces and take the scissors to your fabric!

Following the cutting plan for your fabric width and garment size, pin the pattern pieces to the fabric, then cut out all pieces in fabric and transfer any markings to the fabric (see page 24).

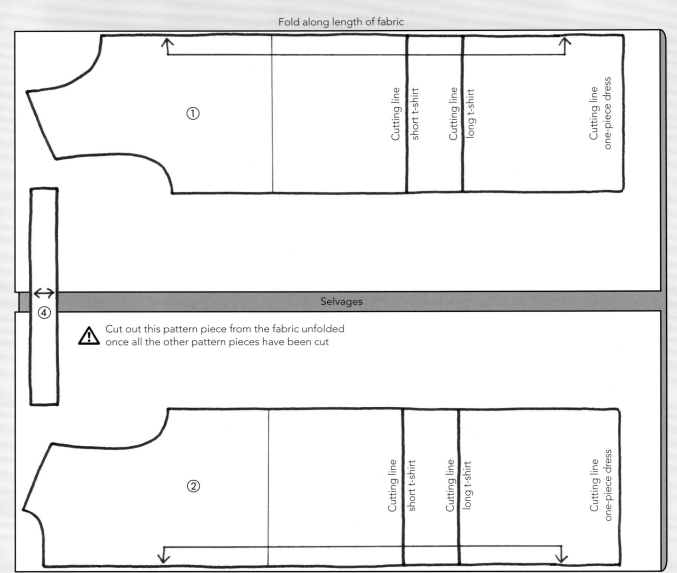

Fold along length of fabric

Cutting line short t-shirt

Cutting line long t-shirt

Cutting line one-piece dress

①

Selvages

④

⚠ Cut out this pattern piece from the fabric unfolded once all the other pattern pieces have been cut

②

Cutting line short t-shirt

Cutting line long t-shirt

Cutting line one-piece dress

Fold along length of fabric

Cutting plan 1a

Pattern pieces

① T-shirt & dress front

② T-shirt & dress back

③ T-shirt & dress sleeve (choose short or long)

④ T-shirt & dress neckband

⑤ T-shirt & dress cuff optional

⑥ Dress contrast band (optional)

Key

Fabric — Right side — Wrong side

Pattern pieces — Printed side up — Printed side down

PREPARING YOUR PATTERN PIECES

Trace off the pattern pieces in the size you need from the pattern sheet. For all versions you will need: T-shirt & dress front, T-shirt & dress back, T-shirt & dress sleeve (short or long), T-shirt & dress neckband

Cuffed-sleeve version: T-shirt & dress cuff

Contrast band version: Dress contrast band

Read the instructions in Using Paper Patterns, page 23.

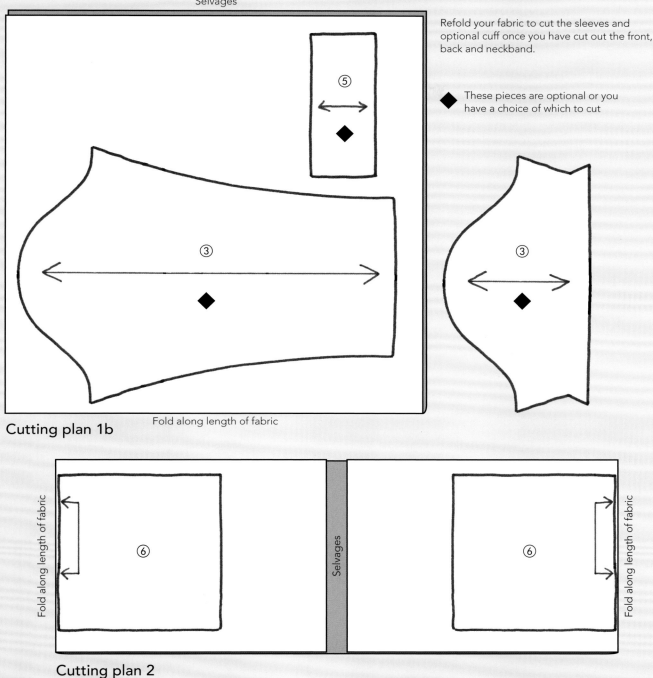

Selvages

Refold your fabric to cut the sleeves and optional cuff once you have cut out the front, back and neckband.

◆ These pieces are optional or you have a choice of which to cut

⑤

③

③

Fold along length of fabric

Cutting plan 1b

Fold along length of fabric

⑥

Selvages

⑥

Fold along length of fabric

Cutting plan 2

Pattern adjustments (read the detailed instructions in Using Paper Patterns, page 24, for how to lengthen your pattern pieces):

● Short T-shirt—trace the front and back body pattern pieces to the length printed on the pattern; no adjustments are needed.

● Long T-shirt—extend the front and back body pattern pieces by 5 in. (12.5 cm).

● Elasticated waist dress (or a plain dress, not shown)—extend the front and back body pattern pieces by 15¾ in. (40 cm).

● Dress with contrast band—extend the front and back body pattern pieces by 16½ in. (42 cm) and cut off the bottom 11½ in. (29 cm) to make the pattern pieces for the band.

● Ankle length dress (not shown)—extend the front and back body pattern pieces by 28¾ in. (73 cm).

● Cuffed sleeve—trace the sleeve to the long sleeve length and remove the hem allowance (1 in./2.5 cm).

PUTTING IT TOGETHER

Seam allowance is ⅜ in. (1 cm)

Hem allowance is 1 in. (2.5 cm)

Key to diagrams

Right side Wrong side

MAKE SURE YOU READ

In order to choose the most suitable machine settings and seam and hem types for your fabric, make sure you read Setting up Your Machine, page 21, Sewing Seams, page 25, and Sewing Hems & Finishing Edges, page 27. Don't forget to "press as you go!"

All plain versions (not the shirred or patchwork versions): joining shoulders, finishing neck, attaching sleeves, stitching side and underarm seams

1 Place the front and back body together with the right sides of the fabric touching. Pin the shoulder seams together, baste (tack), and machine the seam. If you're using very stretchy fabric (such as interlock or rib) or heavy fabric (such as loopback sweat/French terry), it's worth taping the shoulder seams to stop them stretching out of shape (see Special Treatments—Taping Seams, page 32).

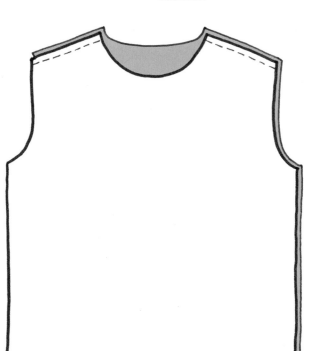

2 Finish the neck using the Folded Band Edging (T-shirt Neck) method, see Sewing Hems & Finishing Edges, page 27.

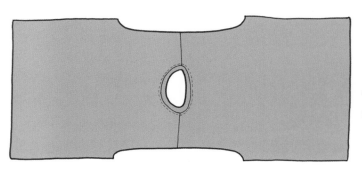

3 Open out the joined front and back T-shirt and place it on a flat surface so that you're looking at the right side of the fabric.

4 Take one of your sleeves and fold it in half along the length. Place a pin in the fold to mark the center of the sleeve head.

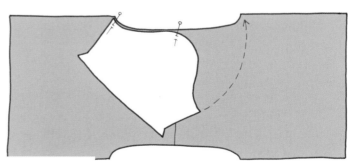

5 Open out the sleeve and place it onto the T-shirt body at the armhole so the right sides of the fabric are touching. Line up the pin in the sleeve head with the shoulder seam in the T-shirt body and pin them together.

6 Bring one end of the sleeve head around to meet the end of the armhole of the body and pin them together. Do the same at the other end.

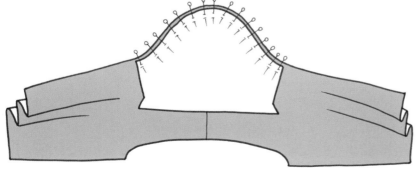

7 Pin the rest of the sleeve to the armhole; you will need lots of pins, placed at right angles to the cut edges of the fabric. Make sure the cut edges of the fabric of the T-shirt body and the sleeve head stay level—the sleeve will try to creep beyond the armhole; don't let it!

8 Baste this seam in place, then machine carefully with the sleeve on top. Keep checking the body of the T-shirt underneath as you sew, to make sure the fabric isn't getting caught and no tucks or wrinkles are being stitched into the seam.

9 Press the seam toward the body of the T-shirt and repeat with the other sleeve.

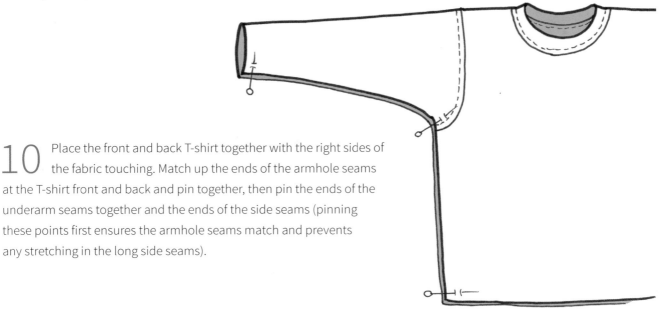

10 Place the front and back T-shirt together with the right sides of the fabric touching. Match up the ends of the armhole seams at the T-shirt front and back and pin together, then pin the ends of the underarm seams together and the ends of the side seams (pinning these points first ensures the armhole seams match and prevents any stretching in the long side seams).

11 Next, pin in between so that the entire underarm and side seams are pinned together on each side of the T-shirt.

12 Baste in place and machine. Press the seam open or toward the back of the T-shirt, depending on which seam you have used.

TIP
If you are making a short sleeve, follow the little kick out wing shape at the end of the underam seams, this gives enough fabric to turn back the hem.

13 Hem as described for All versions: optional cuffs and hemming (step 3 on page 46).

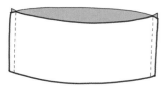

Long-sleeved dress version with contrast band: attaching contrast band

1 Make the upper part of the dress as described for the plain T-shirt and dress, steps 1–12 (pages 46–48).

2 Place the front and back band pieces together with the right sides of the fabric touching. Pin, baste if needed, and machine.

3 With the T-shirt inside out, bring the two side seams together so that you can mark the center front and center back of the T-shirt with pins. Do the same to the top edge of the band section.

TIP

If you're using a fabric with a one-way (directional) print for the band, make sure you're marking the top edge of the contrast band so that your print remains the right way up once your dress is finished!

4 Slot the contrast band inside the T-shirt with the right sides of the fabrics touching, so that the top edge of the band is level with the lower edge of the T-shirt. Pin the side seams of the T-shirt and band together, match the pins marking the center fronts and center backs of the T-shirt and band, and pin them together, then pin the rest of the seam in between. Baste if needed and machine.

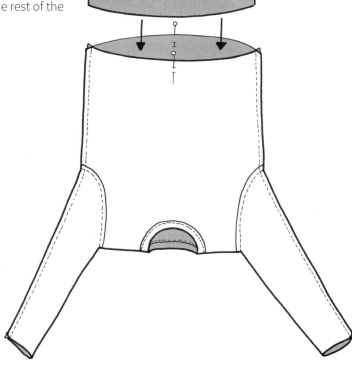

5 Press the seam either open, or up toward the main body of the T-shirt, depending on which seam you have used.

6 Hem as described for All versions: optional cuffs and hemming (step 3).

Short-sleeved dress version with elasticated waist: attaching elastic

1 Make the dress as described for plain T-shirt and dress, steps 1–13 (pages 46–48).

2 Cut a piece of ⅜-in (1-cm) wide elastic long enough to fit your waist, with an additional 1¼ in. (3 cm) for joining the ends.

3 Make sure you have clearly and correctly transferred the markings for the elastic position from the paper pattern onto the wrong side of your fabric.

4 Follow the instructions in Special Treatments—Using Elastic to Gather, page 35, to attach the elastic to your dress.

Long t-shirt version with shirred detail: shirring

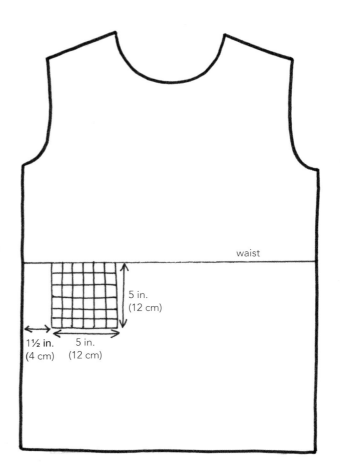

waist

5 in.
(12 cm)

1½ in.   5 in.
(4 cm)   (12 cm)

1   Once you have cut out your fabric, mark the position and
    shape of your shirring on the right side of your fabric. As a
guide, the shirred detail in my sample is on the front T-shirt only,
an area 5 x 5 in. (12 x 12 cm) square, positioned 1½ in. (4 cm) in
from the side seam, as shown below. You can experiment with
different sizes and positions for your shirring.

2   Follow the instructions in Special Treatments—
    Shirring, page 36, to complete your shirred detail.

3   When you have finished shirring, continue
    making the T-shirt as described for the plain
versions, steps 1–13 (pages 46–48).

Short-sleeved t-shirt version with patchwork section: cutting patchwork pieces, piecing patchwork, attaching patchwork section

1 Cut the back T-shirt and sleeves from your main fabric using the pattern pieces traced from the pattern sheets.

2 Trace the front T-shirt pattern from the pattern sheets, mark the center front line, then flip over your paper, align the center front lines, and trace it again to make a full front piece rather than a half front. Draw onto this new whole front pattern piece the lines for your patchwork design and number the individual pieces.

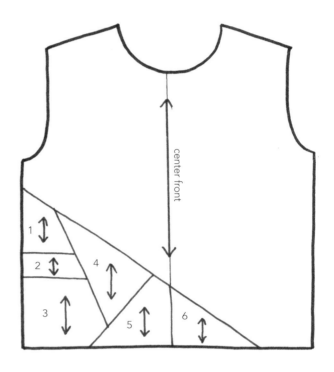

3 Trace each piece of the patchwork separately and remember to add a grainline and seam and hem allowances where needed. Number the pieces to help identify them in the correct order for construction. Cut out the pieces.

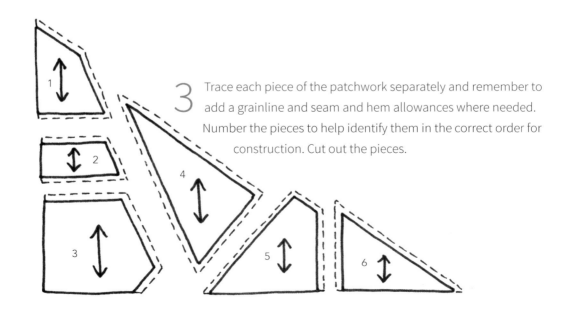

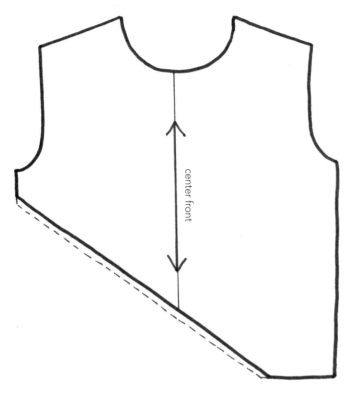

4   Add a seam allowance along the edge of the remaining T-shirt front pattern piece from where you have removed the patchwork section. Cut out the front from your main fabric.

TIP

When cutting the T-shirt front and patchwork pieces from your fabric, make sure you place all the pattern pieces the same way up on the right side of all your fabrics. As the patchwork design is asymmetric, if you swap and change which side of the fabric you place your pattern pieces onto, they won't fit together when you come to sew them.

5   Join the patchwork pieces together in order; 1 to 2, 2 to 3, and so on, use a stretch straight stitch so that you can press the seams open to reduce bulk.

6   Once the patchwork section is complete, attach it to the T-shirt Front. Place the patchwork section onto the T-shirt front with the right sides of the fabrics touching and join along the diagonal seam. Use plenty of pins to prevent either side stretching and to make sure all the seams in the patchwork section remain pressed open.

7   Continue making the T-shirt as described for the plain versions, steps 1–13 (pages 46–48).

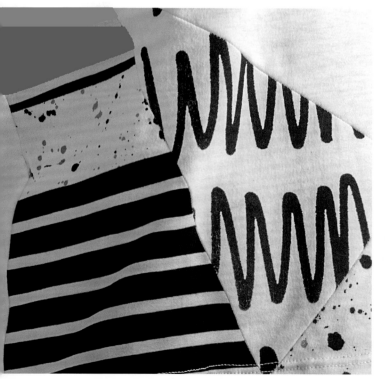

All versions: optional cuffs, hemming

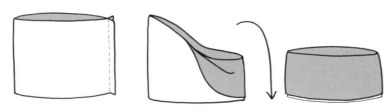

1 If you have chosen to have a cuff at the end of your long sleeves, fold each
   cuff in half along the length with the right sides of the fabric touching and pin
together the notched seam. Machine in place and fold the (now circular) cuffs in
half with the wrong sides of the fabric touching.

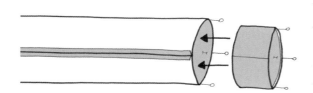

2 Attach the cuffs to the ends of the sleeves as described in
   how to attach the Folded Band Edging (T-shirt Neck), see
Sewing Hems & Finishing Edges, page 27. Divide the circumference
of the cuff into four along the open/cut edge, then pin the cuff
to the right side of the sleeve at these four matching points,
stretching the cuff to fit in between. Make sure the seam in the
cuff lines up with the underarm seam in the sleeve.

3 You can hem the bottoms of the T-shirts and the short
   sleeves with any of the methods in Sewing Hems &
Finishing Edges, page 27, as they don't need to stretch. Use
a simple zig-zag, 3-step zig-zag, or stretch straight stitch to
hem the long sleeves and the bottom edges of the T-shirt
dresses, as they need to be able to stretch.

DERWENT
WIDE LEG TROUSERS

I love wide-legged trousers, especially when they're made from knitted fabric; flattering and comfortable, what's not to like.

These trousers have a deep elastic at the waist used as a facing, which gives a beautiful neat, flat finish, and they sit approximately 1½ in. (4 cm) below the natural waist. There are three length options to choose from: really long, for those blessed with long legs, those who want to wear them with heels or if you want to make super slouchy trousers; a standard length; and a cute cropped length.

Wear these trousers with the Peak T-shirt (page 38) or the Winnats Tank top (page 66) for a laid-back comfortable outfit. Your fabric choice will completely change the finished look; a marl gray ponte roma, like my long pair, can be dressed up with a simple skin-tight black rollneck sweater or dressed down with an easy T-shirt and sneakers. Make a pair in black ponte roma for a smart office look or choose scuba or heavy jersey in the cropped length to wear for yoga practice.

Follow the instructions in Sizing & Taking Measurements (page 12) for exactly where and how to measure yourself and how to choose which size to make.

WITH THESE TROUSERS, YOU WILL PRACTICE THE FOLLOWING BASIC TECHNIQUES:

- Seams

- Hems

- Using elastic as a waist facing

FINISHED TROUSER MEASUREMENTS

Size (Your actual hip measurement)

	34¾ in. (88 cm)	36¼ in. (92 cm)	38 in. (96 cm)	39½ in. (100 cm)	41 in. (104 cm)	43 in. (109 cm)	45 in. (114 cm)	47 in. (119 cm)	49 in. (124 cm)	51 in. (129 cm)
Waist (Approx. 1½ in./ 4 cm below natural waist)	24¼ in. (62 cm)	26 in. (66 cm)	27½ in. (70 cm)	29 in. (74 cm)	30¾ in. (78 cm)	32½ in. (83 cm)	34½ in. (88 cm)	36½ in. (93 cm)	38½ in. (98 cm)	40½ in. (103 cm)
Hips	34 in. (86 cm)	35½ in. (90 cm)	37 in. (94 cm)	38½ in. (98 cm)	40 in. (102 cm)	42¼ in. (107 cm)	44 in. (112 cm)	46 in. (117 cm)	48 in. (122 cm)	50 in. (127 cm)
Inside leg: Long	32¾ in. (83 cm)	32¾ in. (83 cm)	32¾ in. (83 cm)	32¾ in. (83 cm)	32¾ in. (83 cm)	32¾ in. (83 cm)	32¾ in. (83 cm)	32¾ in. (83 cm)	32¾ in. (83 cm)	32¾ in. (83 cm)
Inside leg: Standard	30¼ in. (77 cm)	30¼ in. (77 cm)	30¼ in. (77 cm)	30¼ in. (77 cm)	30¼ in. (77 cm)	30¼ in. (77 cm)	30¼ in. (77 cm)	30¼ in. (77 cm)	30¼ in. (77 cm)	30¼ in. (77 cm)
Inside leg: Cropped	16 in. (41 cm)	16 in. (41 cm)	16 in. (41 cm)	16 in. (41 cm)	16 in. (41 cm)	16 in. (41 cm)	16 in. (41 cm)	16 in. (41 cm)	16 in. (41 cm)	16 in. (41 cm)

WHAT FABRIC SHOULD I USE?

These wide leg trousers will look best in medium-weight knitted fabrics such as ponte roma, scuba, or single jersey (as long as it's not too thin and lightweight).

Does my fabric need to have spandex (elastane)? Yes. What percentage stretch does my fabric need? The fabric needs to contain at least 3% elastane and have at least 50% stretch.

My samples are made in the following fabrics:

• Long leg version: gray marl ponte roma 74% polyester, 23% rayon, 3% spandex.

• Cropped version: navy ponte roma 71% cotton, 24% nylon, 5% spandex.

If you are unsure whether a fabric is suitable, check the Glossary of Fibers & Fabrics(page 120).

PREPARING YOUR PATTERN PIECES

Trace off the pattern pieces in the size you need from the pattern sheet. For all versions you will need: Trouser front, Trouser back. Read the instructions in Using Paper Patterns, page 23.

Pattern adjustments (read the detailed instructions in Using Paper Patterns, page 24, for how to lengthen your pattern pieces):

• Cropped length version—simply trace the pattern pieces to the length printed on the pattern.

• Long or standard length versions—extend the legs of both pattern pieces by 16½ in. (42 cm) to make the long length trousers, or 14¼ in. (36 cm) to make the standard length trousers.

FABRIC REQUIREMENTS

Size (Your actual hip measurement)

	34¾ in. (88 cm)	36¼ in. (92 cm)	38 in. (96 cm)	39½ in. (100 cm)	41 in. (104 cm)	43 in. (109 cm)	45 in. (114 cm)	47 in. (119 cm)	49 in. (124 cm)	51 in. (129 cm)
Long or standard length version										
Fabric width 60 in. (150 cm) or wider	2 yd (1.9 m)	2 yd (1.9 m)	2 yd (1.9 m)	2 yd (1.9 m)	2 yd (1.9 m)	2 yd (1.9 m)	2½ yd (2.2 m)	2½ yd (2.2 m)	2½ yd (2.2 m)	2½ yd (2.2 m)
Cropped version										
Fabric width 60 in. (150 cm) or wider	1⅛ yd (1 m)	1⅛ yd (1 m)	1⅛ yd (1 m)	1⅛ yd (1 m)	1⅛ yd (1 m)	1⅛ yd (1 m)	1⅜ yd (1.2 m)	1⅜ yd (1.2 m)	1⅜ yd (1.2 m)	1⅜ yd (1.2 m)

WHICH CUTTING PLAN TO FOLLOW

Size (Your actual hip measurement)

	34¾ in. (88 cm)	36¼ in. (92 cm)	38 in. (96 cm)	39½ in. (100 cm)	41 in. (104 cm)	43 in. (109 cm)	45 in. (114 cm)	47 in. (119 cm)	49 in. (124 cm)	51 in. (129 cm)
Long or standard length	1	1	1	1	1	1	2	2	2	2
Cropped length	1	1	1	1	1	1	2	2	2	2

YOU WILL NEED

For all versions

Matching sewing thread

3-in. (7.5-cm) wide elastic—enough to fit around your waist

CUTTING YOUR FABRIC

Make sure you read the Preparing Knits for a Project section (page 19) and Using Paper Patterns (page 23) before you lay out your pattern pieces and take the scissors to your fabric!

Following the cutting plan for your fabric width and garment size, pin the pattern pieces to the fabric, then cut out all pieces in fabric and transfer any markings to the fabric (see page 24).

Pattern pieces

① Trouser front
② Trouser back

Key

Fabric

Right side   Wrong side

Pattern pieces

Printed side up   Printed side down

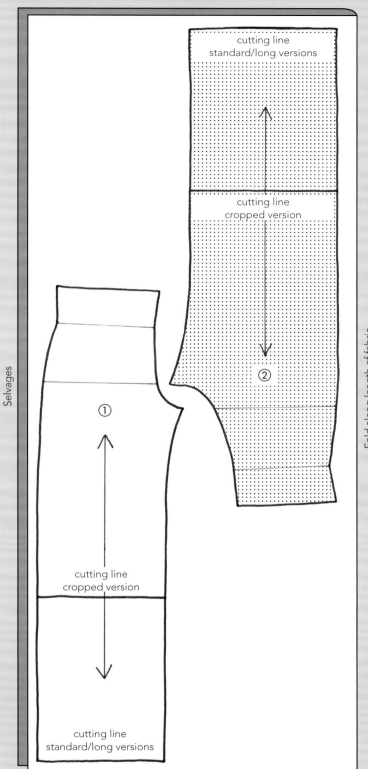

Cutting plan 1

★ Long version—add 2¼ in. (6 cm) to the standard length of both pieces to make the long length trousers.

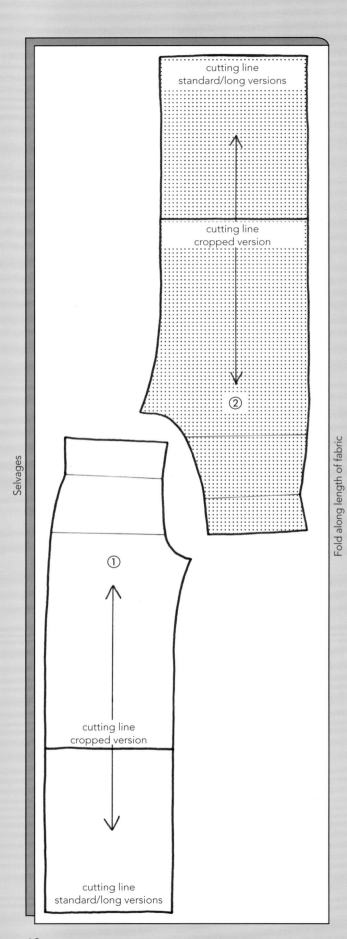

cutting line
standard/long versions

cutting line
cropped version

②

cutting line
cropped version

cutting line
standard/long versions

Selvages

Fold along length of fabric

Cutting plan 2

★ Long version—add 2¼ in. (6 cm) to the standard length of both pieces to make the long length trousers.

Pattern pieces

① Trouser front
② Trouser back

Key

Fabric

Right side   Wrong side

Pattern pieces

Printed
side up   Printed
side down

MAKE SURE YOU READ

In order to choose the most suitable machine settings and seam and hem types for your fabric, make sure you read Setting up Your Machine, page 21, Sewing Seams, page 25, and Sewing Hems & Finishing Edges, page 27. Don't forget to "press as you go!"

PUTTING IT TOGETHER

Seam allowance is ⅜ in. (1 cm)
Hem allowance is 1½ in. (4 cm)

Key to diagrams

Right side   Wrong side

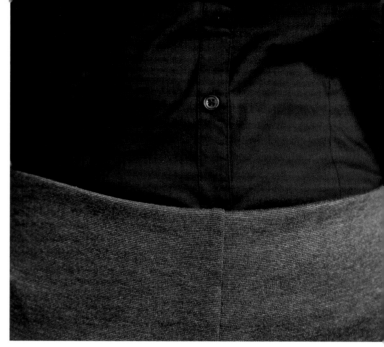

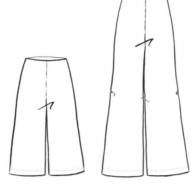

All versions: stitching seams, preparing elastic waist facing, hemming

1 Place the two front legs with right sides touching. Pin the center front seam together (the center front is the curved edge with a single notch). Baste (tack) and machine the seam. Repeat with the two back legs (the center back is the curved edge with a double notch).

2 Open out the joined front and back trousers and place them right sides touching. We're going to join the two inside leg seams in one go. Line up the ends of the center front and center back seams along the inside leg seam and pin them together.

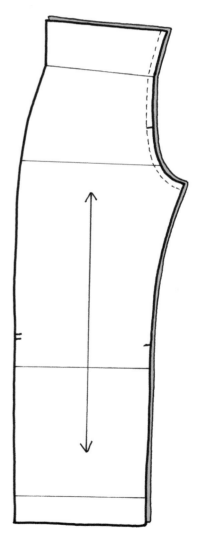

TIP

If you have used a seam that is pressed to one side, it will be easier to keep the center front and center back seams aligned if these seams are pressed in opposite directions to each other.

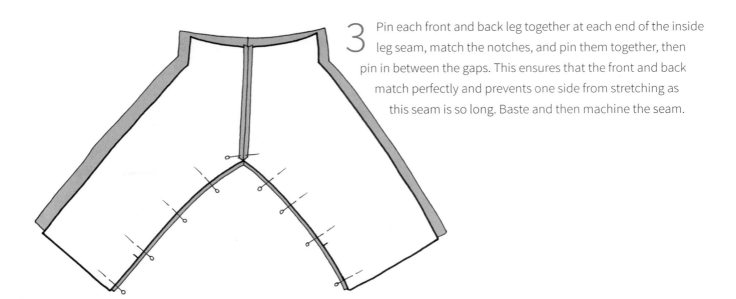

3 Pin each front and back leg together at each end of the inside leg seam, match the notches, and pin them together, then pin in between the gaps. This ensures that the front and back match perfectly and prevents one side from stretching as this seam is so long. Baste and then machine the seam.

4 Pin the front and back together at the side seams with right sides touching, in the same way as the inside leg seam, ie. pin each end of the seams first, then the matched notches, and then the spaces in between. Baste and then machine each side seam. Make sure you follow the exact shaping at the top (waist end) of the side seams, so that the waist facing folds back as intended once the elastic has been attached.

NOTE: The back legs are wider than the fronts so you will need to reposition the legs so that the edges of the side seams are level.

5 Cut your elastic to the following length: the waist measurement from the body measurement chart (see Sizing & Taking Measurements, page 12) for the size you're making (or your actual waist measurement if it's a lot different) PLUS ¾ in. (2 cm) for a seam. The measurement of your lower waist (where the top of the trousers sit) is likely to be bigger than this, but that gives the elastic just the right amount of stretch to be comfortable while still holding up your trousers!

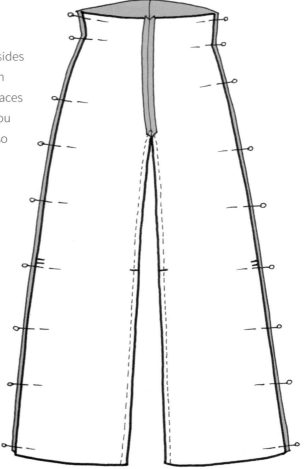

6 Join the cut ends of the elastic using a ⅜-in. (1-cm) seam allowance and a stretch straight stitch (or a regular straight stitch, reinforced by sewing it twice).

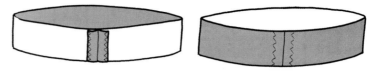

7 Press the seam open. Stitch the seam allowances to the elastic with a zig-zag stitch.

8 You're going to divide this circle of elastic into four: fold the circle of elastic in half with the seam you've just sewn at one side to find the halfway point and insert a pin to mark it. Open out the elastic then fold in half again, this time bringing the pin to touch the seam and place pins in the two folds to mark the quarter-way points.

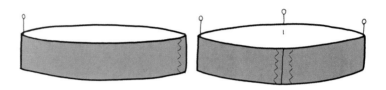

9 The pins in the elastic will match up with the center front, center back, and side seams in your trousers. Attach the elastic following the instructions in Special Treatments—Using Elastic as a Waist Facing, page 32.

10 The hem of these trousers doesn't need to stretch, so you can hem them using any of the four hemming methods in Sewing Hems & Finishing Edges, page 27.

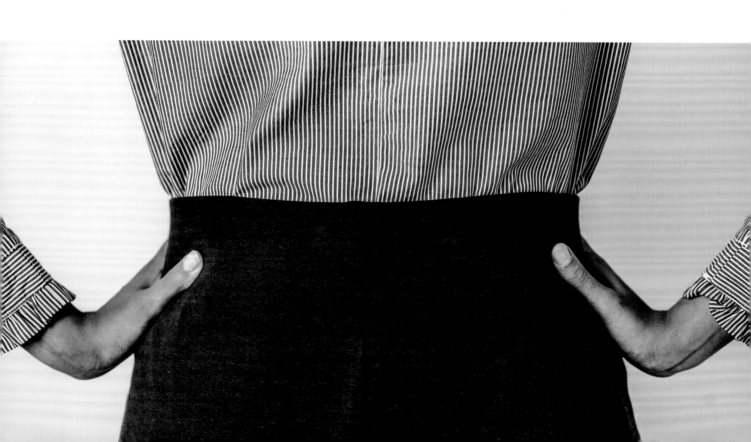

WINNATS TANK

Tank top, vest, call it what you like but this little sleeveless scoop neck top or dress is quick to make, totally wearable, and a great project for practicing the folded band edge finish. What's better, the top version uses just a yard (meter) of fabric.

This pattern adapts to make a vest-length tank top, a knee-length tank dress, or a floor-skimming maxi dress. The fit of the tank is more snug than the Peak T-shirt (page 38) but not tight; it's snug over the bust (with 1½ in./4 cm negative ease so that it stretches to fit), less fitted at the waist and hips, and then drops n a slight A-line shape to the dress lengths, giving you room at the hem to walk comfortably.

The Winnats Tank could quickly make itself an indispensable part of your wardrobe—it can be so many things depending on the fabric you choose; make a vest in a cool drapey viscose single jersey and team it with a pair of Derwent Wide Leg Trousers (page 58) for an easy, dressed-up style, or match a striped vest with the Monsal Lounge Pants (page 78) for exercising. The tank dress in the short and maxi lengths are the perfect easy-wearing summer holiday frocks, and by attaching a vest to the Longshaw Skirt (page 108) you can make a really eye-catching, yet comfortable dress for everyday wear.

If this is one of your first projects using knitted fabrics, choose an easy-to-sew, mid-weight, cotton-rich single jersey and make one of the plain versions. Once you're hooked, try the color-blocked maxi dress and perfect your seam matching skills!

Follow the instructions in Sizing & Taking Measurements (page 12) for exactly where and how to measure yourself and how to choose which size to make.

WITH THIS T-SHIRT, YOU WILL PRACTICE THE FOLLOWING BASIC TECHNIQUES:

- Seams • Hems

- Folded band edging

FINISHED TANK MEASUREMENTS

Size (Your actual bust measurement)

	31½ in. (80 cm)	33 in. (84 cm)	34¾ in. (88 cm)	36¼ in. (92 cm)	38 in. (96 cm)	39¾ in. (101 cm)	41¾ in. (106 cm)	43¾ in. (111 cm)	45¾ in. (116 cm)	47¾ in. (121 cm)
Bust	30 in. (76 cm)	31½ in. (80 cm)	33 in. (84 cm)	34¾ in. (88 cm)	36¼ in. (92 cm)	38¼ in. (97 cm)	40¼ in. (102 cm)	42¼ in. (107 cm)	44 in. (112 cm)	46 in. (117 cm)
Waist	30 in. (76 cm)	31½ in. (80 cm)	33 in. (84 cm)	34¾ in. (88 cm)	36¼ in. (92 cm)	38¼ in. (97 cm)	40¼ in. (102 cm)	42¼ in. (107 cm)	44 in. (112 cm)	46 in. (117 cm)
Hips	33 in. (84 cm)	34¾ in. (88 cm)	36¼ in. (92 cm)	38 in. (96 cm)	39½ in. (100 cm)	41½ in. (105 cm)	43¼ in. 110 (cm)	45¼ in. (115 cm)	47¼ in. (120 cm)	49¼ in. (125 cm)
Back length: Vest	22½ in. (57 cm)	22½ in. (57 cm)	23 in. (58.5 cm)	23 in. (58.5 cm)	23¾ in. (60 cm)	23¾ in. (60 cm)	24¼ in. (61.5 cm)	24¼ in. (61.5 cm)	24¾ in. (63 cm)	24¾ in. (63 cm)
Back length: Short dress	38½ in. (97.5 cm)	38½ in. (97.5 cm)	39 in. (99 cm)	39 in. (99 cm)	39½ in. (100.5 cm)	39½ in. (100.5 cm)	40¼ in. (102 cm)	40¼ in. (102 cm)	40¾ in. (103.5 cm)	40¾ in. (103.5 cm)
Back length" Long dress	50 in. (127 cm)	50 in. (127 cm)	50½ in. (128.5 cm)	50½ in. (128.5 cm)	51¼ in. (130 cm)	51¼ in. (130 cm)	51¾ in. (131.5 cm)	51¾ in. (131.5 cm)	52½ in. (133 cm)	52½ in. (133 cm)

WHAT FABRIC SHOULD I USE?

These tanks work in a wide range of light- to medium-weight knitted fabrics, such as: single jersey, interlock, rib, lighter weight ponte roma, and scuba.

Does my fabric need to have spandex (elastane)? No.
What percentage stretch does my fabric need? The fabric used for the neckband and armhole bands needs to have at least 50% stretch.

If your main fabric doesn't have the required amount of stretch, use ribbing for the neck and armhole bands.

My samples are made in the following fabrics:

• Vest-length tank with black squiggle print: hand-printed 97% cotton, 3% spandex single jersey

• Vest-length tank in cream: 93% viscose, 5% acrylic, 2% polyester confetti effect single jersey

• Vest-length tank in gray: 48% cotton, 48% viscose, 4% polyester confetti effect single jersey

• Short dress striped version: 70% cotton, 18% bamboo, 12% spandex single jersey

• Maxi dress version with contrast panel: main navy and white printed fabric 96% polyester, 4% spandex ponte roma; contrast band 95% polyester, 5% spandex scuba

If you are unsure whether a fabric is suitable, check the Glossary of Fibers & Fabrics (page 120).

PREPARING YOUR PATTERN PIECES

Trace off the pattern pieces in the size you need from the pattern sheet. For all versions you will need: Tank front, Tank back, Tank neckband, Tank armhole band

Pattern adjustments (read the detailed instructions in Using Paper Patterns, page 24, for how to lengthen your pattern pieces):

● Vest-length tank—trace the front and back body pattern pieces to the length printed on the pattern; no adjustments are needed.

● Short dress—extend the front and back body pattern pieces by 16 in. (40.5 cm).

● Maxi plain dress (not shown)—extend the front and back body pattern pieces by 27½ in. (70 cm).

● Maxi dress with contrast panel—extend the front and back body pattern pieces by 27½ in. (70 cm). See instructions for details of how to separate into individual pattern pieces.

FABRIC REQUIREMENTS

Size (Your actual bust measurement)

	31½ in. (80 cm)	33 in. (84 cm)	34¾ in. (88 cm)	36½ in. (92 cm)	38 in. (96 cm)	39¾ in. (101 cm)	41¾ in. (106 cm)	43¾ in. (111 cm)	45¾ in. (116 cm)	47¾ in. (121 cm)
Fabric width										
Vest										
60 in. (150 cm) or wider	1 yd (0.9 m)	1 yd (0.9 m)	1 yd (0.9 m)	1 yd (0.9 m)	1 yd (0.9 m)	1 yd (0.9 m)	1 yd (0.9 m)	1 yd (0.9 m)	1 yd (0.9 m)	1 yd (0.9 m)
Short dress										
60 in. (150 cm) or wider	1½ yd (1.3 m)	1½ yd (1.3 m)	1½ yd (1.3 m)	1½ yd (1.3 m)	1½ yd (1.3 m)	1½ yd (1.3 m)	1½ yd (1.3 m)	1½ yd (1.3 m)	1½ yd (1.3 m)	1½ yd (1.3 m)
Maxi plain dress (not shown)										
60 in. (150 cm) or wider	1¾ yd (1.6 m)	1¾ yd (1.6 m)	1¾ yd (1.6 m)	1¾ yd (1.6 m)	1¾ yd (1.6 m)	1¾ yd (1.6 m)	1¾ yd (1.6 m)	3⅛ yd (2.9 m)	3⅛ yd (2.9 m)	3⅛ yd (2.9 m)
Maxi dress with contrast panel										
60 in. (150 cm) or wider	1½ yd (1.3 m)	1½ yd (1.3 m)	1½ yd (1.3 m)	1½ yd (1.3 m)	1½ yd (1.3 m)	1½ yd (1.3 m)	1½ yd (1.3 m)	2 yd (1.9 m)	2 yd (1.9 m)	2 yd (1.9 m)
Contrast fabric: 60 in. (150 cm) or wider	10 in. (25 cm)	10 in. (25 cm)	10 in. (25 cm)	10 in. (25 cm)	10 in. (25 cm)	10 in. (25 cm)	10 in. (25 cm)	10 in. (25 cm)	10 in. (25 cm)	10 in. (25 cm)

* Not suitable for directional (one-way) prints or fabrics with a pile or surface texture (nap)

WHICH CUTTING PLAN TO FOLLOW

Size (Your actual bust measurement)

	31½ in. (80 cm)	33 in. (84 cm)	34¾ in. (88 cm)	36½ in. (92 cm)	38 in. (96 cm)	39¾ in. (101 cm)	41¾ in. (106 cm)	43¾ in. (111 cm)	45¾ in. (116 cm)	47¾ in. (121 cm)
Vest	1	1	1	1	1	1	1	1	1	1
Short dress	1	1	1	1	1	1	1	1	1	1
Maxi dress	1	1	1	1	1	1	1	2	2	2
Maxi dress with contrast panel										
Main fabric	3	3	3	3	3	3	3	4	4	4
Contrast fabric	5	5	5	5	5	5	5	5	5	5

YOU WILL NEED

For all versions

Matching sewing thread

CUTTING YOUR FABRIC

Make sure you read the Preparing Knits for a Project section (page 19) and Using Paper Patterns (page 23) before you lay out your pattern pieces and take the scissors to your fabric!

Following the cutting plan for your chosen version of the project and your size, pin the pattern pieces to the fabric. Cut out all pieces in fabric and transfer any pattern markings onto the fabric, see Using Paper Patterns (page 24).

Pattern pieces

① Vest & dress front
② Vest & dress back
③ Vest & dress neckband
④ Vest & dress armhole band

Key

Fabric		
Right side	Wrong side	

Pattern pieces		
Printed side up	Printed side down	

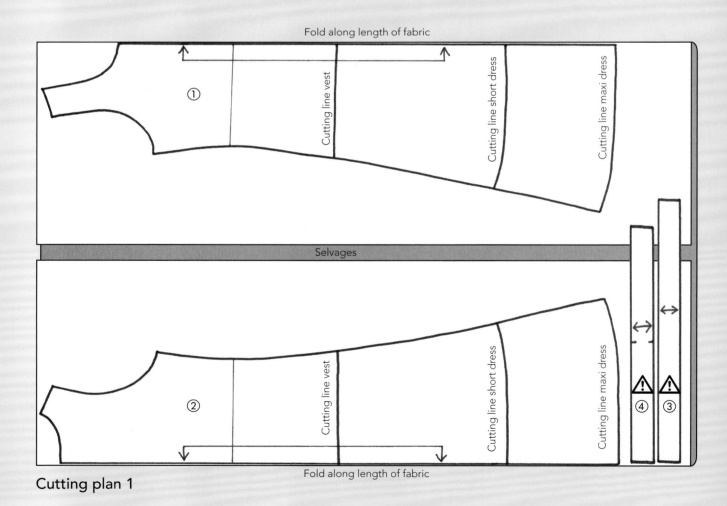

Fold along length of fabric

① Cutting line vest · Cutting line short dress · Cutting line maxi dress

Selvages

② Cutting line vest · Cutting line short dress · Cutting line maxi dress

④ ③

Fold along length of fabric

Cutting plan 1

⚠ Cut out this pattern piece from the fabric unfolded once all the other pattern pieces have been cut

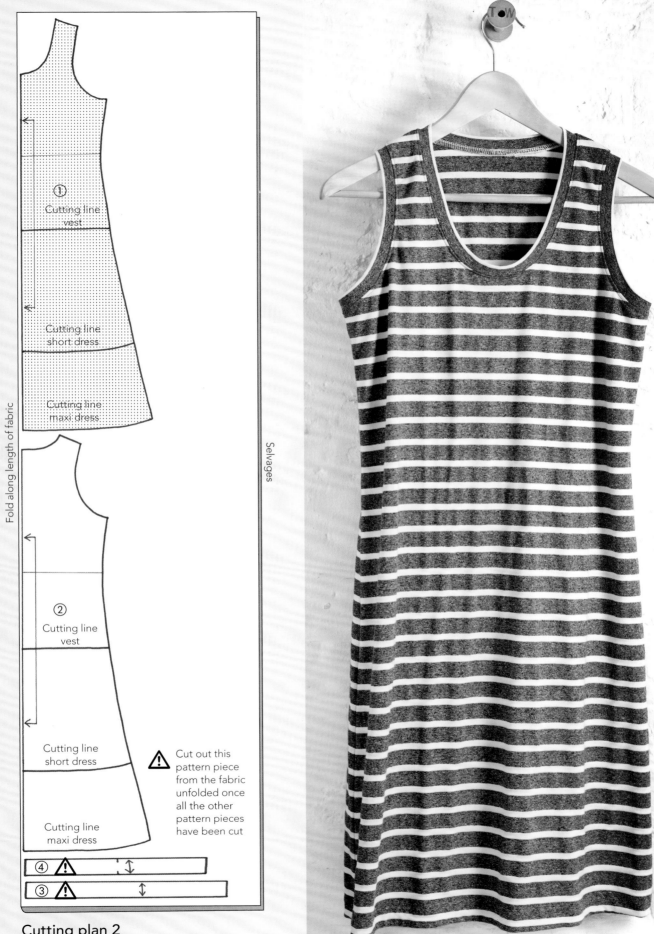

① Cutting line vest

Cutting line short dress

Cutting line maxi dress

Fold along length of fabric

② Cutting line vest

Cutting line short dress

Cutting line maxi dress

⚠ Cut out this pattern piece from the fabric unfolded once all the other pattern pieces have been cut

④ ⚠

③ ⚠

Selvages

Cutting plan 2

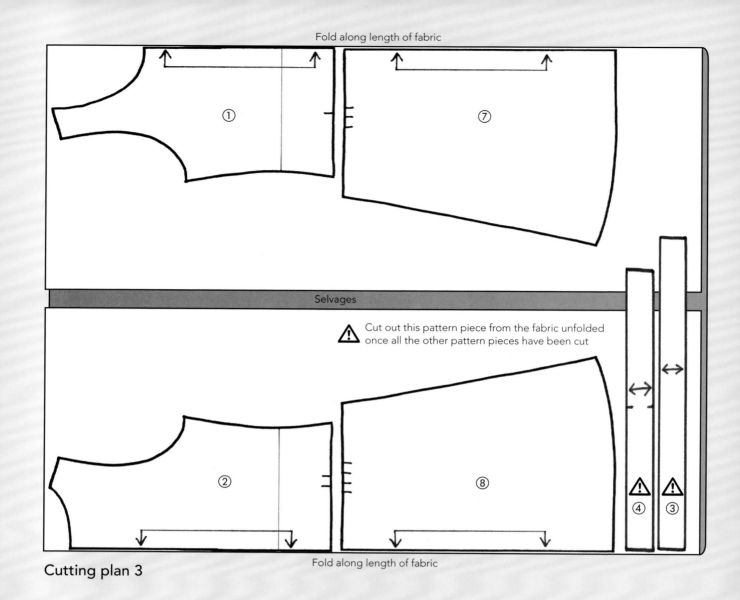

Fold along length of fabric

① ⑦

Selvages

⚠ Cut out this pattern piece from the fabric unfolded once all the other pattern pieces have been cut

② ⑧ ⚠④ ⚠③

Cutting plan 3

Fold along length of fabric

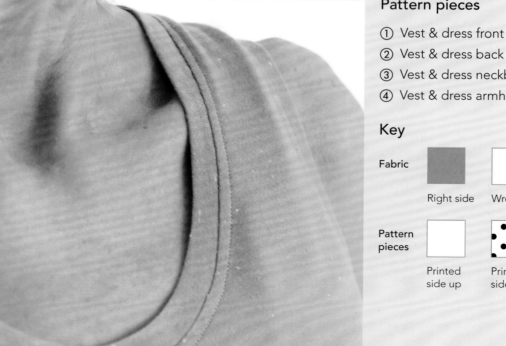

Pattern pieces

① Vest & dress front
② Vest & dress back
③ Vest & dress neckband
④ Vest & dress armhole band

⑤ Dress front contrast panel
⑥ Dress back contrast panel
⑦ Dress lower front
⑧ Dress lower back

Key

Fabric

Right side   Wrong side

Pattern pieces

Printed side up   Printed side down

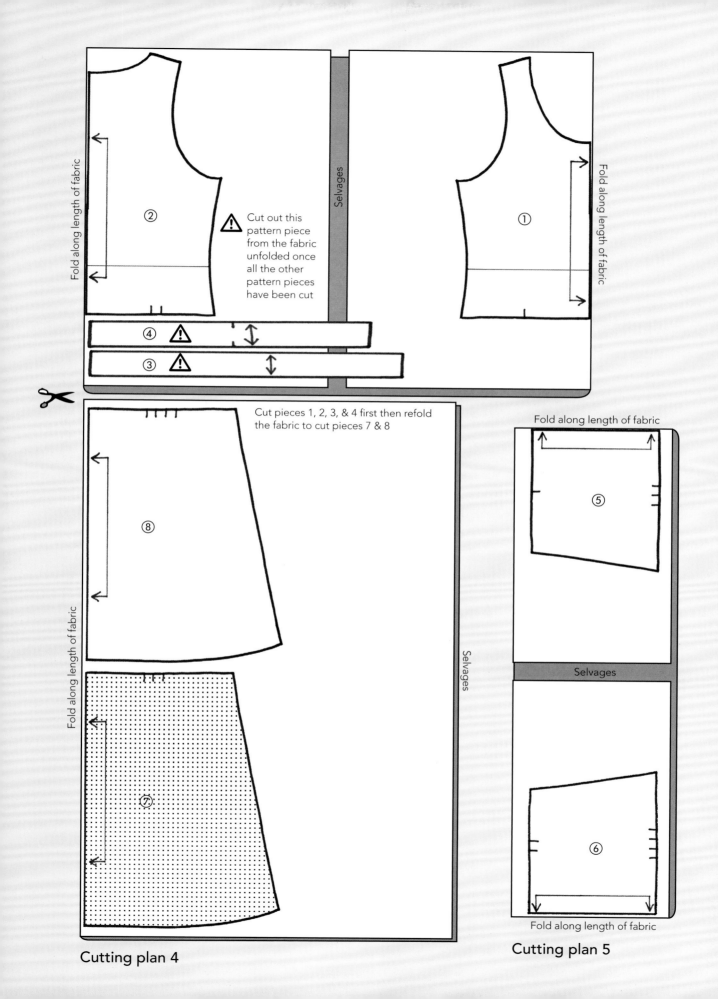

Fold along length of fabric

Selvages

② ⚠ Cut out this pattern piece from the fabric unfolded once all the other pattern pieces have been cut

①

Fold along length of fabric

④ ⚠

③ ⚠

Cut pieces 1, 2, 3, & 4 first then refold the fabric to cut pieces 7 & 8

Fold along length of fabric

⑧

⑦

Selvages

Fold along length of fabric

⑤

Selvages

⑥

Fold along length of fabric

Cutting plan 4

Cutting plan 5

PUTTING IT TOGETHER

Seam allowance is ⅜ in. (1 cm)

Hem allowance is 1 in. (2.5cm)

Key to diagrams

Right side   Wrong side

MAKE SURE YOU READ

In order to choose the most suitable machine settings and seam and hem types for your fabric, make sure you read Setting up Your Machine, page 21, Sewing Seams, page 25, and Sewing Hems & Finishing Edges, page 27. Don't forget to "press as you go!"

All plain versions of vest and dress: joining shoulders, stitching side seams, finishing neck, finishing armholes

1 Place the front and back body together with the right sides of the fabric touching. Pin the shoulder seams together. Baste (tack) and then machine the seam. Press the seam open or toward the back of the tank depending on which seam you have used.

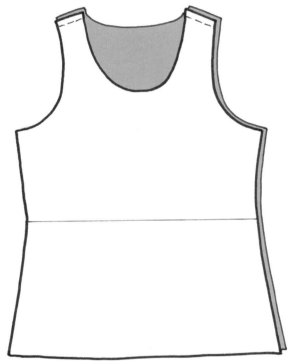

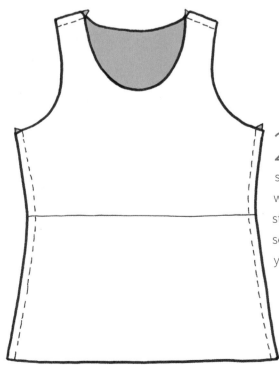

2 Join the front to the back at the side seams. With the right sides of the fabric touching, pin the front to the back along each side seam. Pin each end of the seams first, then match up the notches at the waist and then pin in between. (Pinning these points first prevents any stretching in the long side seams.) Baste in place and machine. Press the seam open or toward the back of the tank depending on which seam you have used.

3 Finish the neck using the Folded Band Edging (T-shirt neck) method (see Sewing Hems & Finishing Edges, page 27). Finish armholes in the same way as neck.

Maxi dress with contrast panel

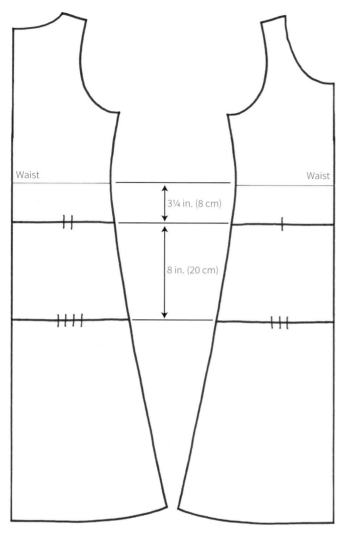

Waist

3¼ in. (8 cm)

8 in. (20 cm)

Waist

1 Once you have extended the front and back body paper pattern pieces by 27½ in. (70 cm), mark the panel lines on both the front and back pattern pieces: mark a line for the upper edge of the panel 3¼ in. (8 cm) below the waistline, mark a line for the lower edge of the panel 8 in. (20 cm) below the first panel line.

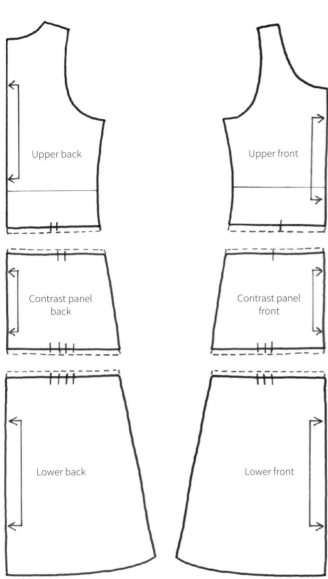

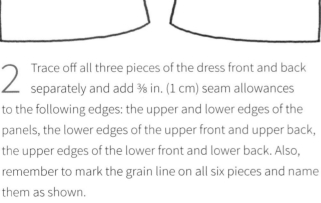

2   Trace off all three pieces of the dress front and back separately and add ⅜ in. (1 cm) seam allowances to the following edges: the upper and lower edges of the panels, the lower edges of the upper front and upper back, the upper edges of the lower front and lower back. Also, remember to mark the grain line on all six pieces and name them as shown.

3   Make the upper part of the dress as described for all plain versions, steps 1–3 (page 74).

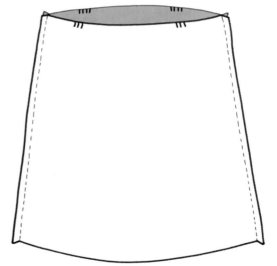

4   Join the side seams of the lower front and lower back dress. With right sides of the fabric touching, pin the front to the back along each side seam. Pin each end of the seams first, then pin in between to prevent stretching. Baste in place and machine. Press the seam open or toward the back of the tank, depending on which seam you have used. Repeat to make the contrast panel.

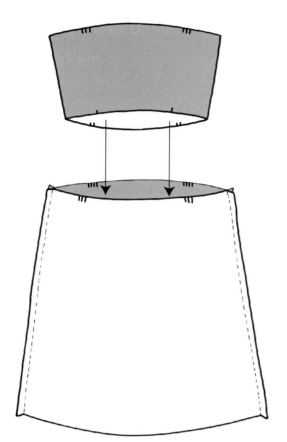

5   With the lower dress inside out and the contrast panel right side out, slot the contrast panel inside the lower dress with the right sides of the fabrics touching. Make sure the triple notches match at the front dress and the four notches match at the back, and pin in place. Then pin together the side seams of the dress and panel, and finally pin the rest of the seam in between. Baste and machine.

6   Press the seam either open, or up toward the main body of the tank, depending on which seam you have used.

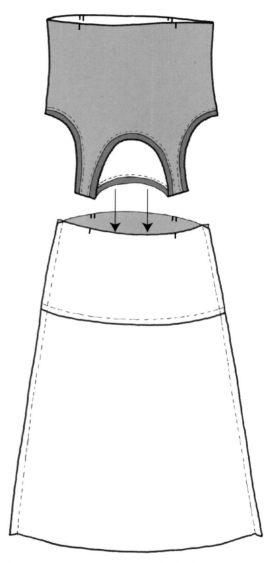

7   Repeat steps 5 and 6 to attach the lower dress and panel to the upper dress. With the lower dress and panel inside out, slot the upper dress inside with right sides of the fabric touching and the single notches lining up at he front and the double notches lining up at the back.

All versions: hemming

Use a simple zig-zag, 3-step zig-zag, or stretch straight stitch to hem the bottoms of the vests and dresses, as they need to be able to stretch (see Sewing Hems & Finishing Edges, page 27.)

MONSAL LOUNGE PANTS

I live in pants like this when I'm relaxing—the first thing I do when I arrive home is change into them. They also make great pyjama bottoms or gym pants, and I'm currently imagining the uncuffed pair in a black drapey bamboo jersey with pockets and a flash of neon band down the legs.

The Monsal Lounge Pants have an elasticated waist (you'll learn two different ways to do this) and have a loose (not baggy), tapering leg shape. The waistband version sits approximately 2 in. (5 cm) below the natural waist; the fold-over elastic version sits a little lower at 3¼ in. (8 cm). There are two length options to choose from: full length, with or without a cuff, and shorts length. The front cut away pockets are optional and I'll show you how to add a flash of color to the pocket openings and side seams with an alternative use for the folded band edging technique. This detail can also help prevent stretching along the pocket opening in lighter weight fabrics.

Team the shorts with the Peak T-shirt (page 38) or Winnats Tank top (page 66), for laid-back loungewear or exercise outfits. Different fabrics can completely change the style of these pants; a completely plain uncuffed pair in a drapey single jersey make a great alternative to leggings; in a denim-effect loopback sweat they'll make a comfortable change from your jeans; and in a super-soft loopback or brushed back heavy sweatshirt (French terry) they're perfect for winter running or just being cozy on the couch.

Follow the instructions in Sizing & Taking Measurements (page 12) for exactly where and how to measure yourself and how to choose which size to make.

> **WITH THESE TROUSERS, YOU WILL PRACTICE THE FOLLOWING BASIC TECHNIQUES:**
>
> - Seams • Hems
> - Using directly attached waist elastic
> - Using elastic in a waistband
> - Folded band edging

FINISHED PANTS MEASUREMENTS

Size (Your actual hip measurement)

	34¾ in. (88 cm)	36¼ in. (92 cm)	38 in. (96 cm)	39½ in. (100 cm)	41 in. (104 cm)	43 in. (109 cm)	45 in. (114 cm)	47 in. (119 cm)	49 in. (124 cm)	51 in. (129 cm)
Waist	31½ in. (80 cm)	33 in. (84 cm)	34¾ in. (88 cm)	36½ in. (92 cm)	38 in. (96 cm)	39¾ in. (101 cm)	41¾ in. (106 cm)	43¾ in. (111 cm)	45¾ in. (116 cm)	47¾ in. (121 cm)
Hips	35½ in. (90 cm)	37 in. (94 cm)	38½ in. (98 cm)	40¼ in. (102 cm)	41¾ in. (106 cm)	43¾ in. (111 cm)	45¾ in. (116 cm)	47¾ in. (121 cm)	49¾ in. (126 cm)	51½ in. (131 cm)
Inside leg: Long (with and without cuffs)	31½ in. (80 cm)	31½ in. (80 cm)	31½ in. (80 cm)	31½ in. (80 cm)	31½ in. (80 cm)	31½ in. (80 cm)	31½ in. (80 cm)	31½ in. (80 cm)	31½ in. (80 cm)	31½ in. (80 cm)
Inside leg: Shorts	13½ in. (34 cm)	13½ in. (34 cm)	13½ in. (34 cm)	13½ in. (34 cm)	13½ in. (34 cm)	13½ in. (34 cm)	13½ in. (34 cm)	13½ in. (34 cm)	13½ in. (34 cm)	13½ in. (34 cm)

My samples are made in the following fabrics:

• Long version in mid blue with white side stripe band: 74% polyester, 23% rayon, 3% spandex ponte roma (contrast side stripe band in same fabric).

• Long version in gray marl with pockets, cuffs, and separate waistbands: main fabric 100% cotton heavy loopback sweat (French terry); waistband, pocket band, and cuffs gray marl ponte roma 74% polyester, 23% rayon, 3% spandex.

• Shorts version in denim blue with pockets and separate waistband: 75% cotton, 25% polyester denim effect loopback sweat (French terry).

If you are unsure whether a fabric is suitable, check the Glossary of Fibers & Fabrics (page 120).

PREPARING YOUR PATTERN PIECES

Trace off the pattern pieces in the size you need from the pattern sheet. Read the instructions in Using Paper Patterns, page 23.

For plain versions with directly attached waist elastic: Pants front (plain without pockets), Pants back.

For long version with cuffs, pockets, and separate waistband: Pants front (with pocket opening), Pants back, Front facing/under pocket bag, Top pocket bag, Pocket band, Waistband, Cuff.

For shorts with pockets: Pants front (with pocket opening) traced to shorts length, Pants back traced to shorts length (make sure you trace the wing shapes at the shorts hem of the side and inside leg seams of both legs), Front facing/under pocket bag, Top pocket bag, Waistband.

No pattern adjustments are needed for this project; all the pattern pieces required are printed to size on the pattern sheets.

WHAT FABRIC SHOULD I USE?

These pants will look best in almost any knitted fabric as long as it's not too thin and see through!

Does my fabric need to have spandex (elastane)?
Main fabric & optional waistband—Not essential, but at least 3% spandex content will help stop your pants "bagging" around the knees if it does.

What percentage stretch does my fabric need?
Fabric for optional cuffs—the fabric used for the cuffs should have at least 50% stretch.
If your main fabric doesn't have the required amount of stretch, choose a contrast fabric with the right amount of stretch for the cuffs.

FABRIC REQUIREMENTS

Size (Your actual hip measurement)

	34¾ in. (88 cm)	36¼ in. (92 cm)	38 in. (96 cm)	39½ in. (100 cm)	41 in. (104 cm)	43 in. (109 cm)	45 in. (114 cm)	47 in. (119 cm)	49 in. (124 cm)	51 in. (129 cm)
Fabric width										
Full length pants without pockets										
60 in. (150 cm) or wider	1⅝ yd (1.4 m)	1⅝ yd (1.4 m)	1⅝ yd (1.4 m)	1⅝ yd (1.4 m)	1⅝ yd (1.4 m)	1⅝ yd (1.4 m)	1⅝ yd (1.4 m)	1⅝ yd (1.4 m)	1⅝ yd (1.4 m)	1⅝ yd (1.4 m)
Full length pants with pockets and cuffs										
Main fabric 60 in. (150 cm) or wider	1⅜ yd (1.25 m)	1⅜ yd (1.25 m)	1⅜ yd (1.25 m)	1⅜ yd (1.25 m)	1⅜ yd (1.25 m)	1⅜ yd (1.25 m)	1⅜ yd (1.25 m)	1⅜ yd (1.25 m)	1⅜ yd (1.25 m)	1⅜ yd (1.25 m)
Contrast fabric 60 in. (150 cm) or wider	14 in. (35 cm)	14 in. (35 cm)	14 in. (35 cm)	14 in. (35 cm)	14 in. (35 cm)	14 in. (35 cm)	14 in. (35 cm)	14 in. (35 cm)	14 in. (35 cm)	14 in. (35 cm)

If using just one fabric (no contrast) add the fabric requirements together.

	34¾ in. (88 cm)	36¼ in. (92 cm)	38 in. (96 cm)	39½ in. (100 cm)	41 in. (104 cm)	43 in. (109 cm)	45 in. (114 cm)	47 in. (119 cm)	49 in. (124 cm)	51 in. (129 cm)
Shorts with pockets										
60 in. (150 cm) or wider	1¼ yd (1.1 m)	1¼ yd (1.1 m)	1¼ yd (1.1 m)	1¼ yd (1.1 m)	1¼ yd (1.1 m)	1¼ yd (1.1 m)	1¼ yd (1.1 m)	1¼ yd (1.1 m)	1¼ yd (1.1 m)	1¼ yd (1.1 m)

WHICH CUTTING PLAN TO FOLLOW

Size (Your actual hip measurement)

	34¾ in. (88 cm)	36¼ in. (92 cm)	38 in. (96 cm)	39½ in. (100 cm)	41 in. (104 cm)	43 in. (109 cm)	45 in. (114 cm)	47 in. (119 cm)	49 in. (124 cm)	51 in. (129 cm)
Full length without pockets	1	1	1	1	1	1	1	1	1	1
Full length with pockets & cuffs—Main fabric	2	2	2	2	2	2	2	2	2	2
Full length with pockets & cuffs —Contrast fabric	3	3	3	3	3	3	3	3	3	3
Shorts with pockets	4	4	4	4	4	4	4	4	4	4

CUTTING YOUR FABRIC

Make sure you read the Preparing Knits for a Project section (page 19) and Using Paper Patterns (page 23) before you lay out your pattern pieces and take the scissors to your fabric!

Following the cutting plan for your fabric width and garment size, pin the pattern pieces to the fabric, then cut out all pieces in fabric and transfer any markings to the fabric (see page 24).

YOU WILL NEED

For all versions

Matching sewing thread

1¼in. (3 cm) wide elastic—enough to fit around your waist

For pocket versions:

½ yd (0.5 m) fusible stay tape or ½ yd (0.5 m) long strip of
fusible interfacing cut to ⅜ in. (1 cm) wide

Pattern pieces

① Pants front

② Pants back

③ Front facing / under pocket bag

④ Top pocket bag

⑤ Waistband

⑥ Cuff

⑦ Pocket band

Key

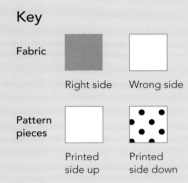

	Fabric	
	Right side	Wrong side

	Pattern pieces	
	Printed side up	Printed side down

Selvages

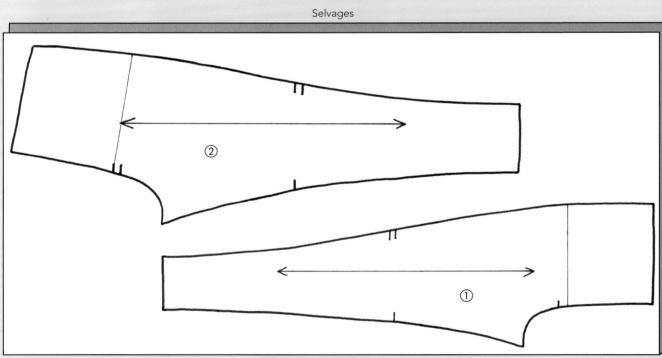

Cutting plan 1

Fold along length of fabric

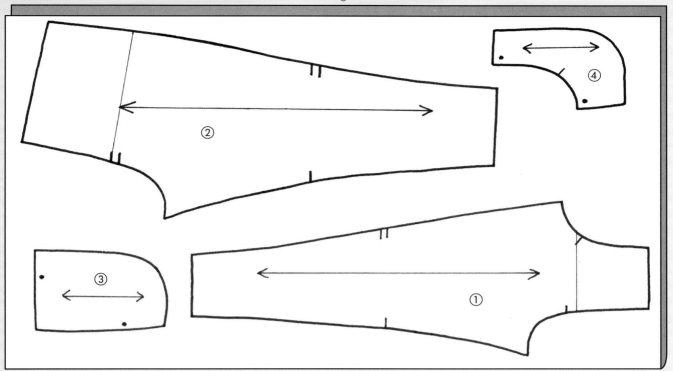

② ④ ③ ①

Cutting plan 2

Fold along length of fabric

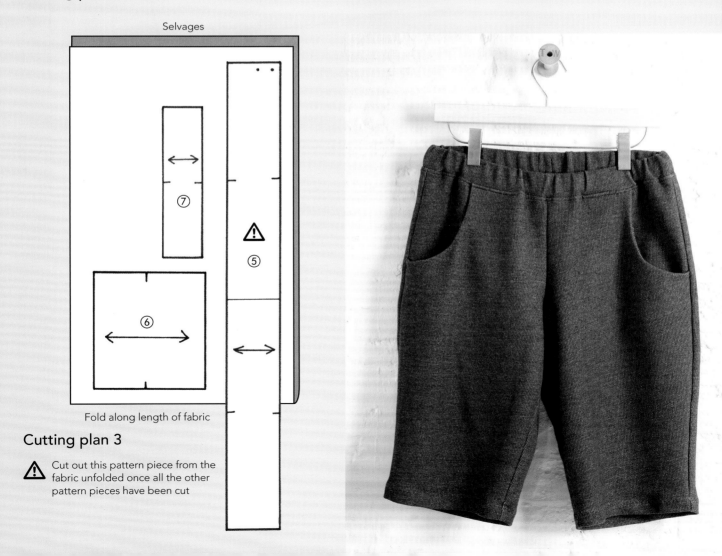

⑦ ⚠ ⑤ ⑥

Fold along length of fabric

Cutting plan 3

⚠ Cut out this pattern piece from the fabric unfolded once all the other pattern pieces have been cut

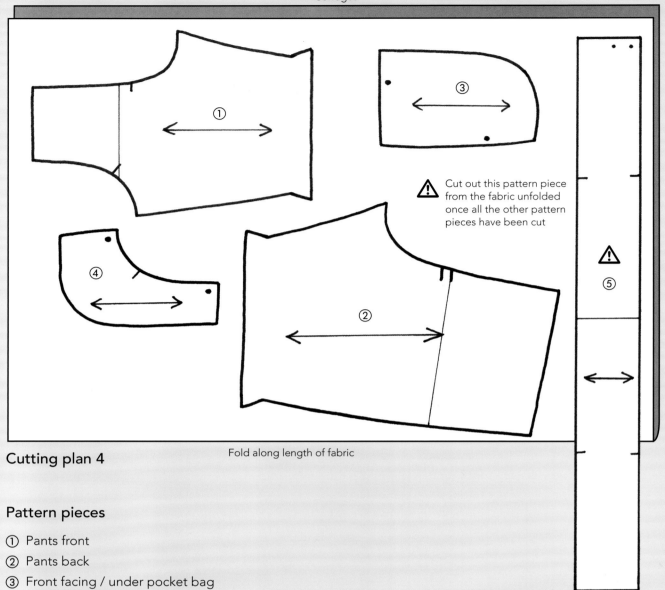

Cut out this pattern piece from the fabric unfolded once all the other pattern pieces have been cut

Fold along length of fabric

Cutting plan 4

Pattern pieces

① Pants front
② Pants back
③ Front facing / under pocket bag
④ Top pocket bag
⑤ Waistband

Key

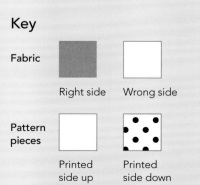

Fabric

Right side   Wrong side

Pattern pieces

Printed side up   Printed side down

MAKE SURE YOU READ

In order to choose the most suitable machine settings and seam and hem types for your fabric, make sure you read Setting Up Your Machine, page 21, Sewing Seams, page 25, and Sewing Hems & Finishing Edges, page 27. Don't forget to "press as you go!"

PUTTING IT TOGETHER

Seam allowance is ⅜ in. (1 cm)
Hem allowance is 1 in. (2.5 cm)

Key to diagrams

Right side   Wrong side

All versions: stitching center front, center back, and inside leg seams

1 Place the two front legs with the right sides of the fabric touching. Pin the center front seam together (the center front is the curved edge with a single notch). Baste (tack) and machine the seam. Repeat with the two back legs (the center back is the curved edge with a double notch). Press the seams open or to one side depending on which seam you have used.

2 Open out the joined front and back pants and place them with the right sides of the fabric touching. We're going to join the two inside leg seams in one go. Line up the ends of the center front and center back seams along the inside leg seam and pin them together.

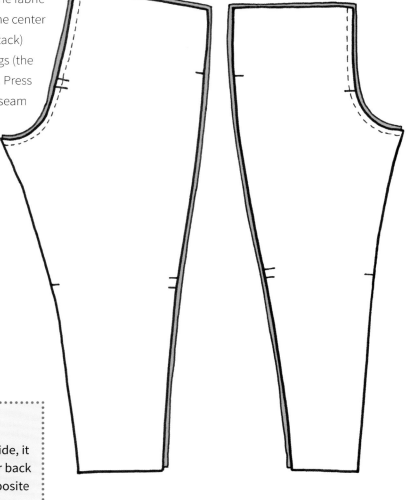

> **TIP**
>
> If you have used a seam that is pressed to one side, it will be easier to keep the center front and center back seams aligned if these seams are pressed in opposite directions to each other.

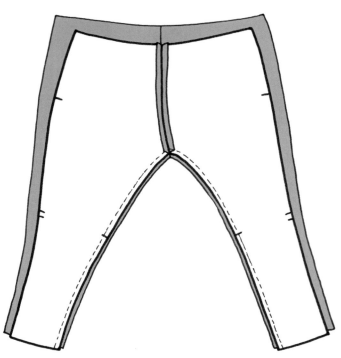

3   Pin each front and back leg together at each end of the inside leg seam, match the notches and pin them together, then pin in between the gaps. This ensures that the front and back match perfectly and prevents one side from stretching as this seam is so long. Baste and then machine the seam.

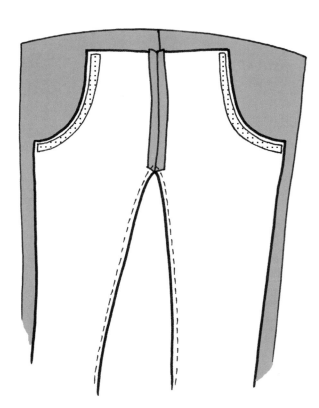

All pocket versions: attaching pockets

1   Iron a strip of fusible stay tape or a cut strip (approximately ⅜ in./1 cm wide) of regular fusible interfacing and iron onto the wrong side of the seam allowances of the front pocket opening edges. Center the tape over the seam line—this prevents the pocket opening edge from stretching, see Special Treatments—Taping Seams, page 32.

Optional pocket band

2 (If you don't want to add pocket bands skip this step and continue to step 4.) To add contrast bands to the pocket openings, fold your two pocket bands in half along the length with wrong sides of fabric touching and press.

3 Place each folded band along the pocket opening edge of each front leg with the right sides of the fabric touching; have all three raw edges of fabric level, match the notches, and pin in place. Bring each end of the band around to meet each end of the pocket opening and pin in place (the band may need a slight stretch as it is a little shorter than the pocket opening), then pin in between. Machine baste the band in place just inside the seam line (approximately 5⁄16 in./0.8 cm in from the raw edge).

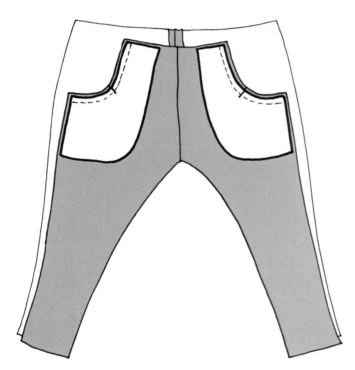

4 Place each top pocket bag onto each front pant leg with right sides of fabric touching and pin along the curved pocket opening edge, matching the notches. (If you added a pocket band this will now be sandwiched in between the pants front and the top pocket bag.) Baste and machine in place.

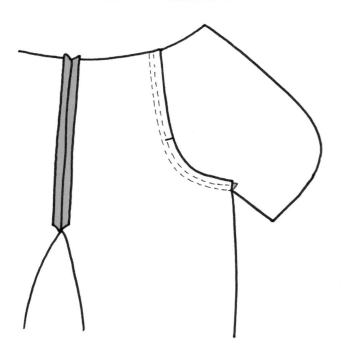

5 Press the seam toward the pocket bag and understitch from the wrong side of the fabric—machine a line of straight stitch approximately ¼ in. (0.5 cm) in from the seam line through both seam allowances and the pocket bag to encourage the seam line to roll in toward the inside of the pocket when the pocket has been constructed.

6 Lay the pants wrong side up, then fold the top pocket bags over along the previous seam line, so that the front pants and top pocket bags are wrong sides touching and you're looking at the right side of the top pocket bags.

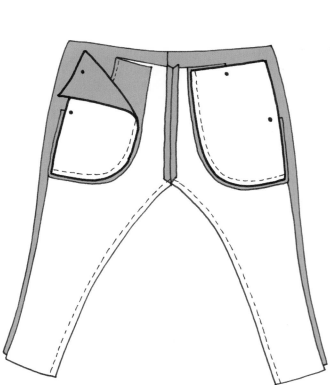

7 With right sides touching and matching the dots, pin each front facing and under pocket bag onto each top pocket bag. Machine the two layers together around the curved edges of the pocket only—make sure you don't also sew through the trouser leg!

8 Baste the pocket in position across the front waist and front side-seam edges.

All versions: joining side seams without contrast band

Pin the front and back legs together at the side seams with right sides of the fabric touching, in the same way as the inside leg seam—pin each end of the seams first, then match the notches, and then pin together the spaces in between. Baste and then machine each side seam.

NOTE: The back legs are wider than the fronts so you will need to reposition the legs so that the edges of the side seams are level.

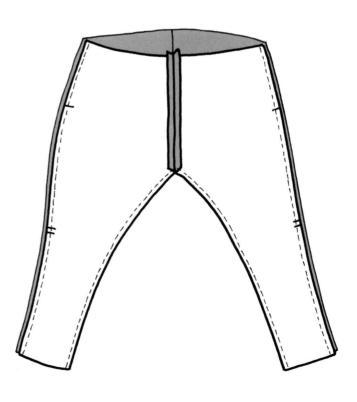

All versions: joining side seams with optional contrast band

1 To add contrast bands to the side seams, cut two lengthwise strips of fabric the length of the side seam and 1½ in. (4 cm) wide. Fold the strips in half along the length with wrong sides of the fabric touching and press.

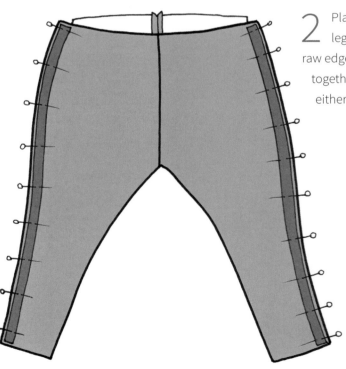

2 Place each folded band along the side seam edge of the back leg with the right sides of the fabric touching, have all three raw edges of fabric level, pin each end of the seam edge and band together first, and then pin in between taking care not to stretch either edge.

3 Machine baste the band in place just inside the seam line (approximately ⁵⁄₁₆ in./0.8 cm in from the raw edge).

4 Continue to join the side seams as described in 'All versions: joining side seams without contrast band' (page 89), with the contrast bands sandwiched in between the front and back leg.

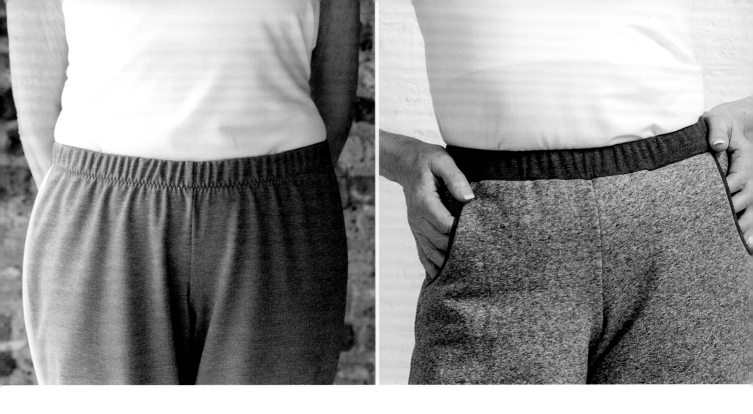

All versions: preparing waist elastic

1 Cut enough elastic to fit your waist. Measure yourself where the pants are going to sit; remember, the waistband version sits 2 in. (5 cm) below the natural waist; the fold-over elastic waist facing sits 3¼ in. (8 cm) below the natural waist. The elastic should be stretched to fit your waist, the amount it's stretched is up to you and what feels comfortable. Add ¾ in. (2 cm) to the length to allow for a seam to join the elastic.

Directly attached waist elastic:

2 To finish the waist of your pants with directly attached waist elastic, see Special Treatments—Elasticated Waist Directly Applied, page 33.

Elastic in a separate waistband:

3 To make and attach a separate waistband, see Special Treatments—Using Elastic in a Waistband, page 34.

Cuffed version: making and attaching cuffs

1 With right sides of the fabric touching, fold each cuff in half and pin together the notched seam. Machine and press. You now have a tube. Fold each cuff in half with the wrong sides of the fabric touching, bringing one raw edge over to meet the other raw edge. Press.

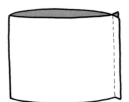 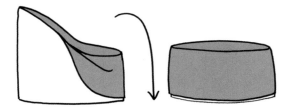

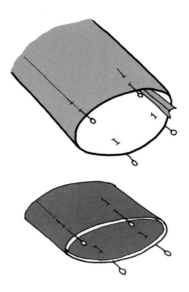

2 Divide the circumference of each hem of the pants into four, using the inside leg seam as one of the quarter points, and mark with pins. Do the same with each cuff.

3 With the pants inside out, slot each cuff inside each pant leg so that the right sides of the fabric are touching and the three cut fabric edges (one on the pants and the two layers of the cuff) are level. Match up and pin the seam in the cuff together with the inside leg seam of the pants, then match up and pin the remaining quarter points marked with pins. Now pin in between; stretch the cuff slightly to fit the rest of the hem and use plenty of pins to hold it in place.

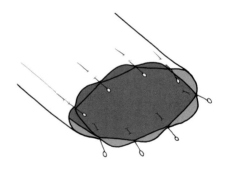

4 Slightly stretch the cuff while machining until the hem of the pants is flat against the cuff. Machine with the cuff layer on top. To do this you need to hold the seam quite firmly in front of the presser foot and behind so that the three layers of fabric are flat and let the machine feed the fabric through and sew while the cuff is stretched.

All other versions: hemming

The hem of the pants and shorts need to stretch, so you will need to use a stretch stitch to sew the hem, see Sewing Hems & Finishing Edges, page 27.

KINDER CARDIGAN

I had been thinking about making the perfect cardigan loosely inspired by kimonos for a long time and so it was an obvious choice to include in this book. It's such a great "between seasons" garment and I've worn the samples I sewed up when developing the pattern almost daily. The Kinder Cardigan is easy to wear and easy and quick to sew. Make yourself one and it will quickly earn its place in your wardrobe as one of your go-to pieces.

You can make the cardigan in three lengths; short, which just skims the hip bone—great teamed with the Derwent Wide Leg Trousers (page 58) or Longshaw Skirt (page 108); mid-length, which comes to just below hip (and yes, covers your rear); or full length, which is just below knee length and looks great with more fitted styles such as skinny jeans, leggings, or the Monsal Lounge Pants (page 78). There is also a choice of short or long sleeves, both finished with a cuff, and for the two longer versions you can add roomy patch pockets. Once you've tackled some basic versions, have a go at mixing and matching fabrics with some color-blocked panel details.

As with all the projects in this book, your choice of fabric can help you create lots of different looks from just this one pattern. Make a mid-length version in loopback sweatshirt/French terry, like my cream version, and team it with jeans for Sunday lounging or spring dog walks. A short cardigan in a metallic knit or drapey viscose or bamboo single jersey, makes an easy cover-up for nights out or special occasions. While the long version, with those bottomless roomy pockets, is just perfect in ponte roma. Once you've made a few, try combining different fabrics; you could make the neckband in a contrasting color or even the sleeves. Mix it up and see what happens!

If this is one of your first projects using knitted fabrics, have a go at a short cardigan in ponte roma, it will be a joy to sew and wear and will get you off to a really good start.

Follow the instructions in Sizing & Taking Measurements (page 12) for exactly where and how to measure yourself and how to choose which size to make.

WITH THIS CARDIGAN, YOU WILL PRACTICE THE FOLLOWING BASIC TECHNIQUES:

- Seams
- Hems
- Patch pockets

FINISHED CARDIGAN MEASUREMENTS

	Size (Your actual bust measurement)				
	31½–33 in. (80–84 cm)	34¾–36¼ in. (88–92 cm)	38–39¾ in. (96–101 cm)	41¾–43¾ in. (106–111 cm)	45¾–47¾ in. (116–121 cm)
Bust	39¾ in. (101 cm)	43 in. (109 cm)	46½ in. (118 cm)	50½ in. (128 cm)	54¼ in. (138 cm)
Sleeve length (short)	10 in. (25.5 cm)	10 in. (25.5 cm)	10 in. (25.5 cm)	10 in. (25.5 cm)	10 in. (25.5 cm)
Sleeve length (long)	21¾ in. (55.5 cm)	22½ in. (57 cm)	23 in (58.5 cm)	23½ in. (60 cm)	24½ in. (61.5 cm)
Back length: short cardigan (down center back from neck seam)	20¼ in. (51.5 cm)	21 in. (53 cm)	21½ in. (54.5 cm)	22 in. (56 cm)	22¾ in. (57.5 cm)
Back length: mid-length	28¼ in. (72 cm)	29 in. (73.5 cm)	29½ in. (75 cm)	30¼ in. (76.5 cm)	30¾ in. (78 cm)
Back length: full-length	38¾ in. (98.5 cm)	39½ in. (100 cm)	40 in. (101.5 cm)	40½ in. (103 cm)	41½ in. (104.5 cm)

WHAT FABRIC SHOULD I USE?

This cardigan works in a wide range of knitted fabrics such as: single jersey, interlock, rib, loopback sweatshirt/French terry, brushed back sweatshirt/fleece, ponte roma, scuba, and sweater knits. Your choice will be based on how warm you want your cardigan to be and what kind of style you're aiming for.

Does my fabric need to have spandex (elastane)? No, due to its loose-fitting style.

What percentage stretch does my fabric need? Again, as the cardigan is a loose fit it will work in even the most stable of knitted fabrics.

My samples are made in the following fabrics:

● Short-sleeved short-length cardigan: main body metallic gray 75% polyester, 21% modal, 4% spandex; printed loopback sweatshirt/French terry contrast panel neon orange 95% polyester, 5% spandex scuba

● Long-sleeved short-length cardigan: gray marl and black 97% viscose, 3% spandex ponte roma

● Long-sleeved mid-length cardigan: cream tweed effect 50% cotton, 48% viscose, 2% acrylic loopback sweatshirt/French terry

● Long-sleeved full-length cardigan: burgundy 97% viscose, 3% spandex ponte roma

If you are unsure whether a fabric is suitable, check the Glossary or Fibers & Fabrics (page 120).

PREPARING YOUR PATTERN PIECES

Trace off the pattern pieces in the size you need from the pattern sheet. For all versions you will need: Cardigan front, Cardigan back, Neckband, Sleeve (short or long), Cuff (for long or short sleeve), Optional pocket.
Read the instructions in Using Paper Patterns, page 23.

Pattern adjustments (read the detailed instructions in Using Paper Patterns, page 24, for how to lengthen your pattern pieces):

• Short cardigan—trace the front and back body and the neckband pieces to the short length printed on the pattern sheet, the short or long sleeve, and the cuff for the short or long sleeve; no adjustments are needed.

• Mid-length cardigan—trace the front and back body and the neckband pieces to the mid-length printed on the pattern sheet. No adjustments are needed.

• Full-length cardigan—extend the mid-length front and back body and neckband pieces as printed on the pattern sheet by 10½ in. (26.5 cm).

• To add contrast panels, see detailed explanation within project instructions.

FABRIC REQUIREMENTS

	Size (Your actual bust measurement)				
	31½–33 in. (80–84 cm)	34¾–36¼ in. (88–92 cm)	38–39¾ in. (96–101 cm)	41¾–43¾ in. (106–111 cm)	45¾–47¾ in. (116–121 cm)
Fabric width	Short cardigan with short sleeves				
60 in. (150 cm) or wider	1⅛ yd (1 m)	1⅛ yd (1 m)	1⅛ yd (1 m)	1½ yd (1.4 m)	1½ yd (1.4 m)
	Short cardigan with long sleeves				
60 in. (150 cm) or wider	1½ yd (1.3 m)	1½ yd (1.3 m)	1½ yd (1.3 m)	1⅞ yd (1.75 m)	1⅞ yd (1.75 m)
	Mid-length cardigan with long sleeves and pockets				
60 in. (150 cm) or wider	1¾ yd (1.6 m)	1¾ yd (1.6 m)	1¾ yd (1.6 m)	2¼ yd (2 m)	2¼ yd (2 m)
	Full-length cardigan with long sleeves and pockets				
60 in. (150 cm) or wider	2 yd (1.9 m)	2 yd (1.9 m)	2 yd (1.9 m)	2½ yd (2.25 m)	2½ yd (2.25 m)

To add contrast panels:
For a contrast panel on the neckband you need 4 in. (10 cm) of contrast fabric
For a contrast panel across the chest you need 6 in. (15 cm) of contrast fabric

WHICH CUTTING PLAN TO FOLLOW

	Size (Your actual bust measurement)				
	31½–33 in. (80–84 cm)	34¾–36¼ in. (88–92 cm)	38–39¾ in. (96–101 cm)	41¾–43¾ in. (106–111 cm)	45¾–47¾ in. (116–121 cm)
All versions	1	1	1	2	2
Contrast panel versions	Follow cutting plans above and cut both fronts or both neckbands with fabric unfolded once all other pieces have been cut. Cut panels from single layer of contrast fabric.				

YOU WILL NEED

For all versions

Matching sewing thread

CUTTING YOUR FABRIC

Make sure you read the Preparing Knits for a Project section (page 19) and Using Paper Patterns (page 23) before you lay out your pattern pieces and take the scissors to your fabric!

Following the cutting plan for your fabric width and garment size, pin the pattern pieces to the fabric, then cut out all pieces in fabric and transfer any markings to the fabric (see page 24).

Key

Fabric

Right side   Wrong side

Pattern pieces

Printed side up   Printed side down

Pattern pieces

1. Cardigan front
2. Cardigan back
3. Cardigan sleeve
4. Cardigan neckband
5. Cardigan pocket
6. Cardigan short sleeve cuff
7. Cardigan long sleeve cuff

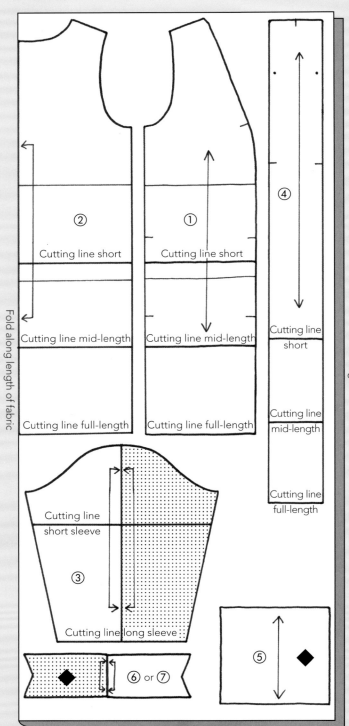

Cutting plan 1

◆ These pieces are optional or you have a choice of which to cut

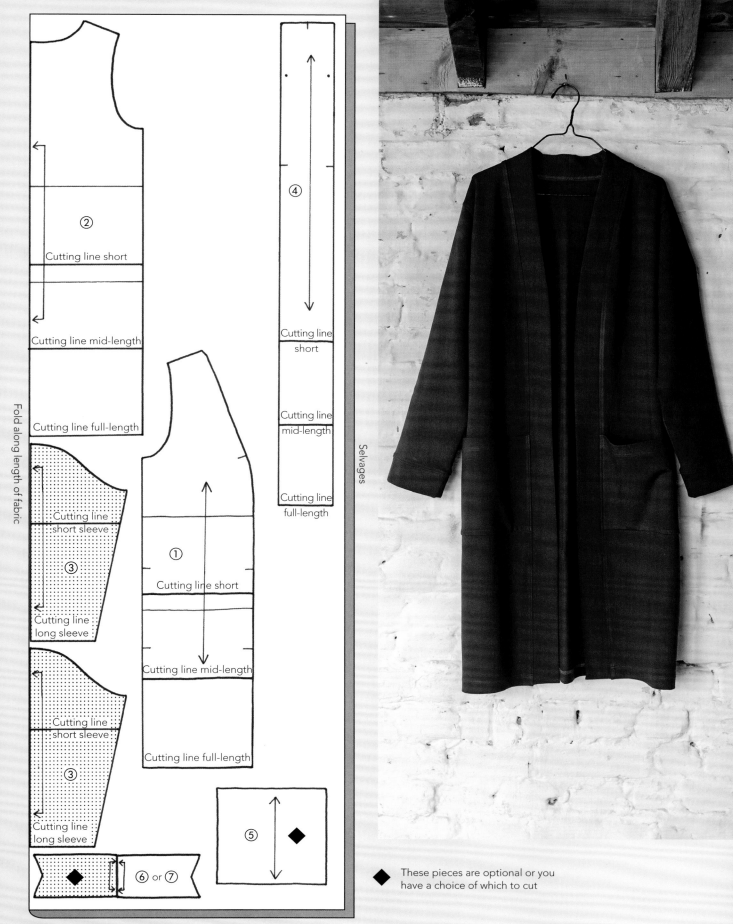

Fold along length of fabric

② Cutting line short

Cutting line mid-length

Cutting line full-length

③ Cutting line short sleeve

Cutting line long sleeve

③ Cutting line short sleeve

Cutting line long sleeve

⑥ or ⑦

① Cutting line short

Cutting line mid-length

Cutting line full-length

④ Cutting line short

Cutting line mid-length

Cutting line full-length

Selvages

⑤

◆ These pieces are optional or you have a choice of which to cut

Cutting plan 2

PUTTING IT TOGETHER

Seam allowance is ⅜ in. (1 cm)
Hem allowance is 1¼ in. (3 cm)

Key to diagrams

Right side

Wrong side

All plain versions without pockets or contrast panels: joining shoulders, attaching neckband, attaching sleeves and cuffs, joining side and underarm seams, hemming

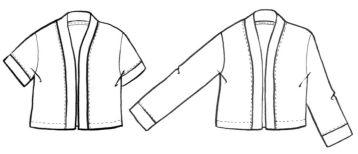

1 Place the front and back body together with the right sides of the fabric touching. Pin the shoulder seams together, baste (tack), and machine the seam. If you're using very stretchy fabric (such as interlock or rib) or heavy fabric (such as loopback sweatshirt/French terry), it's worth taping the shoulder seams to stop them stretching out of shape (see Special Treatments—Taping Seams, page 32).

2 Fold each cuff in half with the right sides of the fabric touching and pin together the short, shaped ends. Machine with a stitch that can be pressed open (for example a stretch straight stitch), in order to reduce the bulkiness of this seam once the cuff is doubled over.

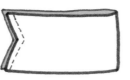

3 Fold the (now circular) cuffs in half with the wrong sides of the fabric touching. Press and baste the open edges together.

4 Place the two neckband pieces together with the right sides of the fabric touching, and pin together the short, notched ends matching the notches. Machine using a stitch that can be pressed open like the cuffs in step 2, to reduce bulk.

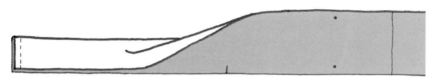

5 Fold the entire neckband in half along the length, with the right sides of the fabric touching. Pin together the short ends and machine.

6 Turn the neckband so that it is right side out and press along the length so that it is now in half with the wrong sides of the fabric touching. Baste the open edges together.

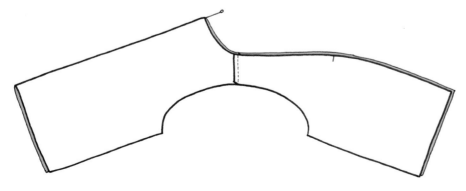

7 Mark the center back neck of the cardigan back with a pin (to find the center back, fold the cardigan back in half and line up the shoulder seams).

8   Lay the cardigan front and back out flat so that you're looking at the right side of the fabric. Place the neckband onto the cardigan and line up the seam in the middle of the neckband with the pin marking the center back neck on the cardigan. Pin together so that the two basted edges of the neckband and the raw edge of the cardigan neck are level.

9   Now match the dots in the neckband with the shoulder seams in the cardigan and pin together. Match the notches in the neckband and the front cardigan and pin together, and place each end of the neckband 1¼ in. (3 cm) above the lower edge of the front cardigan and pin in place.

10 Fold back the 1¼-in. (3-cm) hem allowance at the lower edge of the cardigan front over to cover the end of the neckband, and pin securely. Pin the rest of the neckband in place between the notches and dots and baste securely.

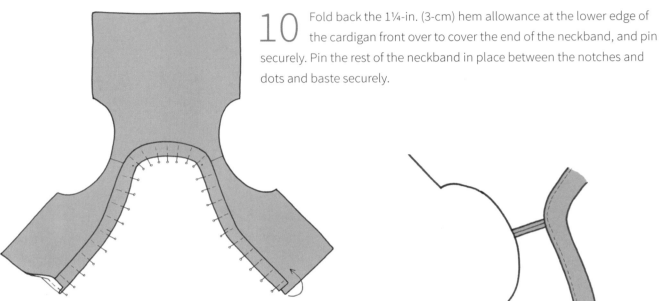

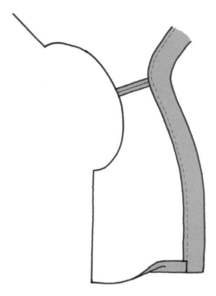

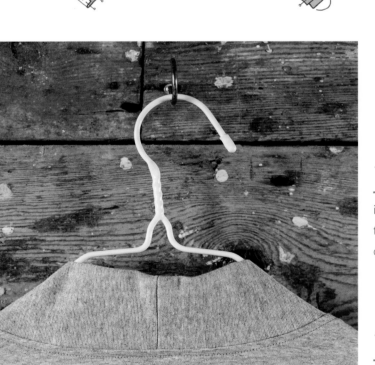

11 Machine in place and turn back the front hem covering the band so that the end of the neckband is now sandwiched in the beginning of the front hem. Press the whole of the seam you have just sewn toward the body of the cardigan, away from the neckband.

12 Open out the cardigan and place it on a flat surface so that you're looking at the right side of the fabric. Attach the sleeves and join the side and underarm seams as described in the Peak T-shirt, steps 4–12 (pages 47–48).

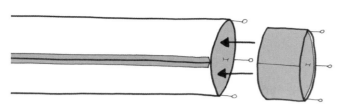

13 Divide the circumference of each cuff into four along the open/cut edge, and divide the circumference of the end of the sleeve into four. Then, with the sleeve inside out, slot the cuff inside the sleeve and pin the cuff to the right side of the sleeve at these four matching points, with all three raw edges level (two in the cuff and one in the sleeve). Make sure the seam in the cuff lines up with the underarm seam in the sleeve. Pin, baste, and machine in place. Press the seam toward the sleeve away from the cuff.

14 Topstitch the neck seam onto the cardigan body and the cuff seams onto the sleeve approximately ¼ in. (5 mm) away from the seam line. Use a straight stitch on a slightly longer than standard stitch length.

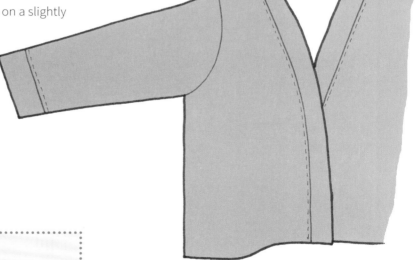

TIP

For thicker fabrics such as loopback sweatshirt/French terry, you may also need to reduce the presser foot pressure or use a walking foot to avoid stretching these bulky seams (see Setting Up Your Machine, page 22, for more information on adjusting the presser foot pressure and using a walking foot).

15 You can hem the bottom of your Cardigan using any of the methods in Sewing Hems & Finishing Edges, page 27, as it doesn't need to stretch.

Cardigans with pockets: making and attaching the pockets

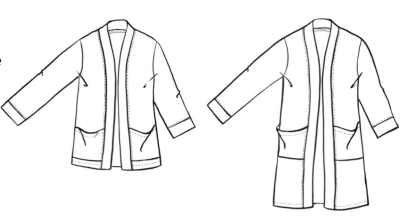

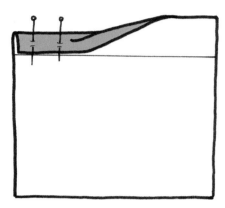

1 Use tailor's chalk to draw a straight line, 2¼ in. (6 cm) in from one of the long edges on each pocket. Fold the long edge over toward the wrong side so that the cut edge of fabric is resting on your chalk line. Press and pin the pocket hem in place, baste if needed.

2 Machine the pocket hem in place using any of the methods in Sewing Hems & Finishing Edges, page 27, as it doesn't need to stretch.

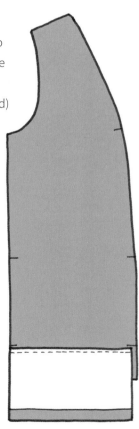

3 Place each pocket bag onto each cardigan front with the right sides of the fabric touching. Position the bottom (un-hemmed) long edge of the pocket level with the lower set of notches on the front edge and side seam of the cardigan front. Pin, baste, and machine in place.

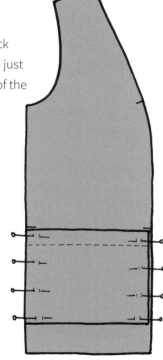

4 Fold the pocket bags back over the seams you have just sewn so that the wrong sides of the pockets are against the right sides of the cardigan fronts, and the hemmed top edges of the pockets are level with the second set of notches on the front edges and side seams of the cardigan fronts. Press and pin the sides of the pockets in place on the cardigan fronts.

5 Follow the instructions for All plain versions steps 1–15 (pages 100–103), to assemble the rest of your cardigan, incorporating the pockets in the neckband seam and in the side seams.

Cardigans with contrast panels: adapting the patterns and attaching the panels

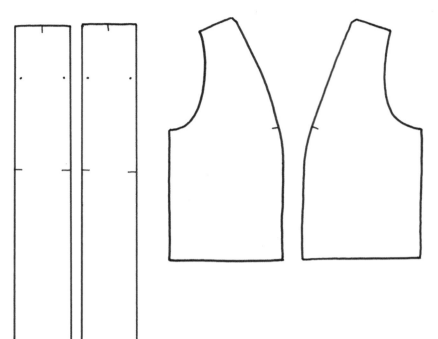

1 Trace the pattern pieces you need from the pattern sheets and trace a second copy of the cardigan front or the cardigan neckband, depending which version of the contrast panel you are doing.

IMPORTANT: if you're adding a contrast panel to the front chest, flip your pattern piece over once you have traced the second front, so that you have a left and right front, and not two identical ones!

2 Mark the position of your contrast panel. As a guide, here are the dimensions I used: for a panel on the front chest—the top of the panel is 2¼ in. (6 cm) below the top of the side seam and is 4½ in. (11 cm) deep; for a panel on the neckband—the top of the panel is 13¾ in. (35 cm) below the center back seam and is 3¼ in. (8 cm) deep. Before tracing off the individual parts of the paneled pattern pieces, mark a single notch on the upper panel seam line and a double notch on the lower panel seam line, to help you put the paneled section together.

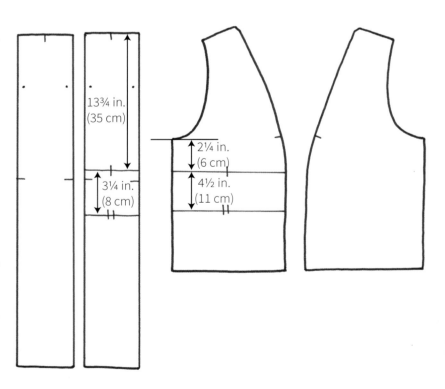

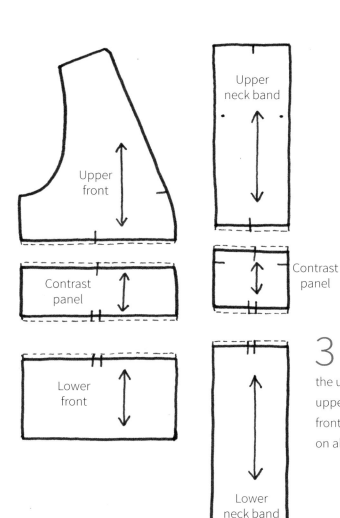

Upper front

Upper neck band

Contrast panel

Contrast panel

Lower front

Lower neck band

3 Trace off each part of the paneled pattern piece separately and add ⅜-in. (1-cm) seam allowances to the following edges: the upper and lower edges of the panels, the lower edges of the upper front or upper neckband, and the upper edges of the lower front and lower neckband. Also, remember to mark the grainlines on all pieces and name them as shown.

4 Once you have prepared your pattern pieces, follow the same cutting plans for the plain versions of the cardigans, but cut both fronts or both neckbands from the fabric unfolded once all other pieces have been cut. Cut your single contrast front or neckband panels from a single layer of contrast fabric, following the grainlines on the pattern pieces.

5 With right sides of the fabric touching, join the panel seams to make a complete front cardigan (press seams open or toward the body, depending on the seam type used), or a complete neckband (on the neckband panel use a stretch straight stitch that can be pressed open to reduce bulk once the band is folded in half).

6 Continue making the cardigan as described for All plain versions, steps 1–15 (pages 100–103).

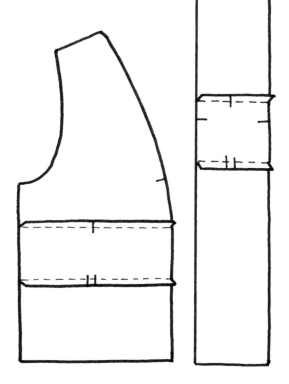

LONGSHAW SKIRT

The Longshaw Skirt is an unusual and bold design that creates a flattering, curvy silhouette and once you've made and worn one, you will realize how comfortable it is and how versatile the design can be.

This skirt is deceptively simple in its construction, being made from just two pieces of fabric plus the waistband, and it sews up really quickly. It has a comfortable, wide elasticated waist and the skirt tapers to the hem, but isn't restrictive to walk in and there are two length options to choose from: just on the knee or below the knee. You can make the skirt with or without the deep pockets cleverly hidden within the draped sides, and I'll also show you how to attach the Longshaw Skirt to the Peak T-shirt or the Winnats Tank (pages 38 and 66), to make some fabulous dresses.

You can dress the Longshaw Skirt up or down to suit different occasions with your choice of fabric. Create a stunning Romanesque skirt or dress by choosing a lighter weight fabric, such as bamboo or viscose single jersey, to really show off the draped detail. In heavier fabrics, such as ponte roma, scuba, or lightweight loopback sweatshirt/French terry, the draped effect is more sculptural and would make a cool dress or skirt to wear to a wedding or special event. Team a short gray marl version with sneakers and a simple Winnats Tank vest for summer days, or make a long black ponte roma version to wear with a stripy long-sleeved Peak T-shirt teamed with leggings and ankle boots for winter.

Follow the instructions in Sizing & Taking Measurements (page 12) for exactly where and how to measure yourself and how to choose which size to make.

WITH THIS SKIRT, YOU WILL PRACTICE THE FOLLOWING BASIC TECHNIQUES:

- Seams
- Hems
- Using elastic in a waistband

FINISHED SKIRT MEASUREMENTS

		Size (Your actual waist measurement)									
		25¼ in. (64 cm)	26¾ in. (68 cm)	28¼ in. (72 cm)	30 in. (76 cm)	31½ in. (80 cm)	33½ in. (85 cm)	35½ in. (90 cm)	37½ in. (95 cm)	39¼ in. (100 cm)	41½ in. (105 cm)
Waist		24½ in. (62 cm)	26 in. (66 cm)	27½ in. (70 cm)	29 in. (74 cm)	30¾ in. (78 cm)	32¾ in. (83 cm)	34¾ in. (88 cm)	36½ in. (93 cm)	38½ in. (98 cm)	40½ in. (103 cm)
Hips		55 in. (140 cm)	56¾ in. (144 cm)	58¼ in. (148 cm)	60 in. (152 cm)	61½ in. (156 cm)	63¼in. (161 cm)	65¼ in. (166 cm)	67¼ in. (171 cm)	69¼ in. (176 cm)	71¼ in. (181 cm)
Length (down center back from top of waistband)	**Short**	22 in. (55.5 cm)	22 in. (55.5 cm)	22 in. (55.5 cm)	22 in. (55.5 cm)	22 in. (55.5 cm)	22 in. (55.5 cm)	22 in. (55.5 cm)	22 in. (55.5 cm)	22 in. (55.5 cm)	22 in. (55.5 cm)
	Long	25¾ in. (65.5 cm)	25¾ in. (65.5 cm)	25¾ in. (65.5 cm)	25¾ in. (65.5 cm)	25¾ in. (65.5 cm)	25¾ in. (65.5 cm)	25¾ in. (65.5 cm)	25¾ in. (65.5 cm)	25¾ in. (65.5 cm)	25¾ in. (65.5 cm)

WHAT FABRIC SHOULD I USE?

The Longshaw Skirt (or dress) looks great in light to medium-weight knitted fabric such as: single jersey, interlock, rib, lighter weight ponte roma, scuba.

Lighter weight knits such as single jersey, will emphasize the draping at the sides, a heavier knit such as ponte roma or scuba will create a more structured, sculptural shape.

Does my fabric need to have spandex (elastane)? No.

What percentage stretch does my fabric need? Your fabric needs to have at least 30% stretch for the top of the skirt to stretch over the hips when it is pulled on.

My samples are made in the following fabrics:

• Short skirt in gray marl: 100% cotton single jersey

• Long skirt in denim-effect fabric: 75% cotton, 25% polyester lightweight loopback sweatshirt/French terry

• Short-sleeved T-shirt dress: 96% polyester, 4% Lycra printed ponte roma

• Tank dress: 60% polyester, 37% viscose, 3% spandex hand-painted ponte roma

If you are unsure whether a fabric is suitable, check the Glossary of Fibers & Fabrics (page 120).

PREPARING YOUR PATTERN PIECES

Trace off the pattern pieces in the size you need from the pattern sheet. Read the instructions in Using Paper Patterns, page 23.

For all skirts you will need: Skirt front and back, Waistband.

For the dresses you will need the relevant Peak T-shirt or Winnats Tank pattern pieces in addition to the skirt pieces.

Pattern adjustments (read the detailed instructions in Using Paper Patterns, page 24, for how to lengthen your pattern pieces):

- Short skirt—trace the skirt front and back pattern piece to the length printed on the pattern; to make the skirt without pockets, fold back the pocket section along the marked fold line.

- Long skirt—extend the skirt front and back pattern piece by 4 in. (10 cm) at the hem.

- Dress made with Peak T-shirt or Winnats Tank—trace the T-shirt or tank front and back pattern pieces to 4¾ in. (12 cm) below the marked waistline.

FABRIC REQUIREMENTS

Size (Your actual waist measurement)

	25¼ in. (64 cm)	26¾ in. (68 cm)	28¼ in. (72 cm)	30 in. (76 cm)	31½ in. (80 cm)	33½ in. (85 cm)	35½ in. (90 cm)	37½ in. (95 cm)	39¼ in. (100 cm)	41½ in. (105 cm)
Fabric width					Short skirt					
60 in. (150 cm) or wider	2 yd (1.9 m)	2 yd (1.9 m)	2 yd (1.9 m)	2 yd (1.9 m)	2 yd (1.9 m)	2 yd (1.9 m)	2 yd (1.9 m)	2 yd (1.9 m)	2 yd (1.9 m)	2 yd (1.9 m)
					Long skirt					
Main fabric 60 in. (150 cm) or wider	2⅜ yd (2.1 m)	2⅜ yd (2.1 m)	2⅜ yd (2.1 m)	2⅜ yd (2.1 m)	2⅜ yd (2.1 m)	2⅜ yd (2.1 m)	2⅜ yd (2.1 m)	2⅜ yd (2.1 m)	2⅜ yd (2.1 m)	2⅜ yd (2.1 m)
					Tank dress					
60 in. (150 cm) or wider	3 yd (2.8 m)	3 yd (2.8 m)	3 yd (2.8 m)	3 yd (2.8 m)	3 yd (2.8 m)	3 yd (2.8 m)	3 yd (2.8 m)	3 yd (2.8 m)	3 yd (2.8 m)	3 yd (2.8 m)
				Short-sleeved T-shirt dress						
60 in. (150 cm) or wider	3⅜ yd (3 m)*	3⅜ yd (3 m)*	3⅜ yd (3 m)*	3⅜ yd (3 m)*	3⅜ yd (3 m)*	3⅜ yd (3 m)*	3⅜ yd (3 m)*	3⅜ yd (3 m)*	3⅜ yd (3 m)*	3⅜ yd (3 m)*

* add an extra 16 in. (40 cm) for a long dress with long sleeves

WHICH CUTTING PLAN TO FOLLOW

Size (Your actual waist measurement)

	25¼ in. (64 cm)	26¾ in. (68 cm)	28¼ in. (72 cm)	30 in. (76 cm	31½ in. (80 cm)	33½ in. (85 cm)	35½ in. (90 cm)	37½ in. (95 cm)	39¼ in. (100 cm)	41¼ in. (105 cm)
All skirts Versions	1	1	1	1	1	1	1	1	1	1
Tank dress	1 for skirt & follow relevant cutting plan for Winnats Tank (page 66)									
Short- or Long-sleeved T-shirt dress	1 for skirt & follow relevant cutting plan for Peak T-shirt (page 38)									

YOU WILL NEED

For all versions

Matching sewing thread

For skirts:

1¼-in. (3-cm) wide elastic—enough to comfortably fit your waist

For dresses:

⅜-in. (1-cm) wide elastic—enough to comfortably fit your waist

CUTTING YOUR FABRIC

Make sure you read the Preparing Knits for a Project section (page 19) and Using Paper Patterns (page 23) before you lay out your pattern pieces and take the scissors to your fabric!

Following the cutting plan for your fabric width and garment size, pin the pattern pieces to the fabric, then cut out all pieces in fabric and transfer any markings to the fabric (see page 24).

Key

Fabric

Right side   Wrong side

Pattern pieces

Printed side up

Pattern pieces

① Skirt front and back

② Waistband

⚠ Cut out this pattern piece from the fabric unfolded once all the other pattern pieces have been cut

Cutting plan 1

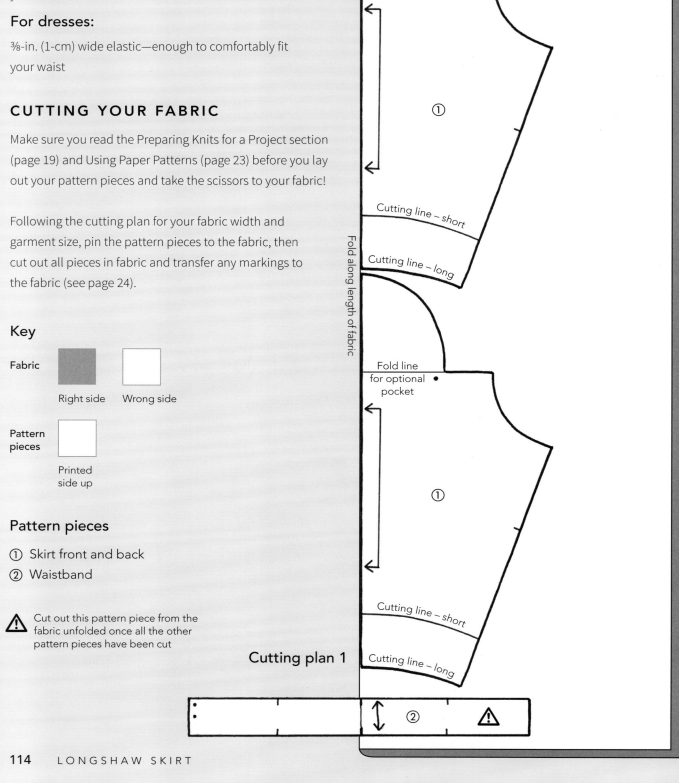

PUTTING IT TOGETHER

Seam allowance is ⅜ in. (1 cm)

Hem allowance is ⅝ in. (1.5 cm)

Key to diagrams

Right side   Wrong side

MAKE SURE YOU READ

In order to choose the most suitable machine settings and seam and hem types for your fabric, make sure you read Setting up Your Machine, page 21, Sewing Seams, page 25, and Sewing Hems & Finishing Edges, page 27. Don't forget to "press as you go!"

All skirts: stitching center front, center back, side seams, making waistband

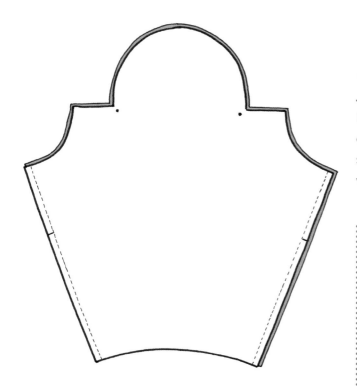

1 Place the two skirt pieces together with the right sides of the fabric touching. Pin the center front and center back seams together (the center seams are the straight edges with a single notch). Baste (tack) and machine the seam. Press the seams open or to one side depending on which seam you have used.

TIP

Pin each end of the seams first, then match the notches, and finally pin in between—this prevents one side of the seam from stretching.

2 Pull the two layers of the skirt apart (still with right sides touching), so that the center back and center front seams are lying on top of each other. Pin together the side seams and around the optional pockets. Baste and machine each seam, pivoting at the dot to sew around the pockets if you have chosen to include them (above left). For a skirt without pockets, simply join the straight side seams, matching up the dots (above right).

3 Cut enough elastic to fit your waist. Measure yourself where the skirt is going to sit (it's designed to sit on your natural waist). The elastic should be stretched to fit your waist, the amount it's stretched is up to you and what feels comfortable. Add ¾ in. (2 cm) to the length to allow for a seam to join the elastic.

4 To make and attach your waistband, see Special Treatments—Elasticated Waist—in a Waistband, page 34.

5 The hem of the skirt needs to stretch, so you will need to use a stretch stitch to sew the hem, see Sewing Hems & Finishing Edges, page 27.

All dresses: attaching top, attaching elasticated waist

1 Make the skirt following All skirts, steps 1 and 2. Make the Peak T-shirt (page 38) or Winnats Tank (page 66), as described in the relevant project instructions, but don't hem the bottom edge.

2 Mark the center front and center back of the T-shirt or tank with pins by folding the garment in half so that the side seams align, then place a pin along each fold to mark the center back and front.

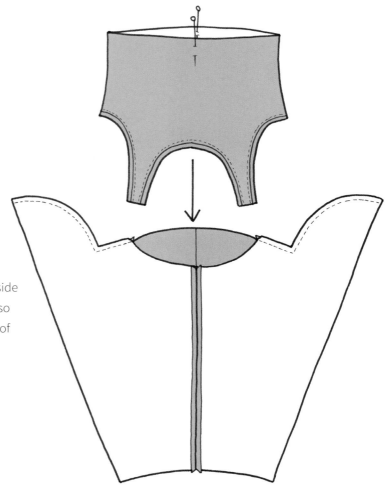

3 With the skirt inside out and the T-shirt or tank right side out, slot the T-shirt or tank inside the skirt neck first, so that the right sides of the fabric are touching and the hem of the T-shirt or tank and the waist edge of the skirt are level.

4 Line up the side seams in the T-shirt or tank with the side seams in the skirt and pin them together, then line up the pins marking the center front and center back of the T-shirt or tank with the center seams in the skirt and pin them together.

TIP

If you have used seams that are pressed to one side, it will be easier to keep the side seams of the skirt and top aligned if these seams are pressed in opposite directions to each other.

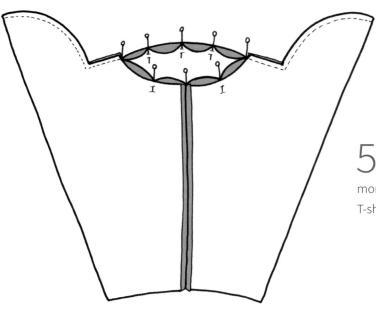

5 Stretch the skirt to fit the T-shirt or tank in between the side seams, center back, and center front and insert more pins. You will need to stretch the skirt more to fit the T-shirt than the tank as the T-shirt is a looser fit.

6 Machine the waist seam, slightly stretching as you sew so that both sides of the seam are the same length and lie flat against each other. Make sure the raw edges of the seam stay level and you don't allow one side to creep out.

7 Cut a piece of ⅜-in (1-cm) wide elastic long enough to comfortably fit your waist, with an additional 1¼ in. (3 cm) for joining the ends.

8 Follow the instructions in Special Treatments—Using Elastic to Gather, page 35, to attach the elastic to the waist seam of your dress.

TIP

Insert your pins at right angles to the cut edge of the fabric—you can fit in more pins and they will hold your fabric more securely while you're stretching the skirt waist to fit.

GLOSSARY OF FIBERS & FABRICS

FIBERS AND FABRICS *Yes they are different things!*

A fiber is the raw material that a fabric is made up of, such as cotton. A fabric is the resulting cloth that can be made in lots of different ways, such as single jersey. The best way to explain the difference is with an example: Cotton Single Jersey and Viscose Single Jersey—they are the same "type" of fabric (single jersey), but made from different fibers (one cotton, one viscose) and so will have slightly different properties and feel different to wear. As you begin to make your own clothes, it is important to learn about the properties of different fibers so that you can start to choose the most appropriate fabrics for what you're making.

This Glossary is split into two sections: a list of the common fibers used in knitted fabrics and a list of the most commonly used knitted fabrics. A quick reference chart of what garments and styles each fabric is best suited for, along with the key properties of each fiber, is included in Know Your Knits, page 16.

Common fibers:

Acrylic A man-made fiber often used as an inexpensive substitute for wool and blended with other fibers such as wool and cotton.

Bamboo A natural fiber made from bamboo plants, which makes a fabric that feels and behaves a lot like cotton; being soft and absorbent. It has a reputation as a sustainable natural fiber as most bamboo fiber is organic and it needs much less water than cotton to grow. Can be machine washed and dried.

Cotton A natural fiber from the cotton plant, it is absorbent, but can take a long time to dry. It creases, but is soft and strong, which makes it popular for clothing worn next to the skin as well as clothes that need to withstand some wear and tear. Organic cotton is becoming much more widely available and is a preferable choice over conventional cotton. Can be machine washed and dried.

Linen A natural fiber that comes from the flax plant that is absorbent and dries quickly, making it cool to wear. It's stronger than cotton, so good for garments subject to some wear and tear. Can be machine washed and dried.

Modal Known as a regenerated fiber, Modal is a type of rayon made from wood pulp—usually from beech trees. Modal is a brand name for this particular type of rayon. It looks and feels like a very smooth soft cotton, is very absorbent, and is often mixed with cotton. Can be machine washed and dried at a low heat.

Nylon A man-made fiber that originates from oil. It is strong, can be wind and water resistant, and dries quickly, making it popular for use in outdoor and sports clothing and accessories. As it is sensitive to heat it must be washed and ironed on a low temperature. It isn't absorbent and so can be uncomfortable to wear in hot weather.

Polyester Another man-made fiber originating from oil. It is strong and water resistant, so dries quickly. Because Polyester is crease-resistant it is often blended with other fibers such as cotton. It isn't absorbent and so can be uncomfortable to wear in hot weather. Can be machine washed and dried on a low heat.

Rayon Similar to viscose, rayon is a regenerated fiber made from wood pulp. It can be made to mimic most natural fibers, commonly silk, cotton, and linen. It is smooth with good drape and very absorbent, but doesn't dry quickly. It must be washed at lower temperatures and is often labeled "dry clean only."

Silk The strongest natural fiber, made from the cocoon of the silk worm. The fibers are extremely long, making it a lustrous fiber that creates very drapey fabrics. Silk fabrics are susceptible to moths, especially if stored unclean. Silk is best washed very gently by hand with a specialist gentle detergent with minimum agitation; don't soak silk and don't leave it damp, creased, and crumpled. Don't tumble dry!

Spandex (known as elastane in Europe) An elastic, man-made fiber often mixed with other fibers to improve stretch and stretch recovery. The higher the elastane content in your fabric, the stretchier it will be. Also known as Lycra, although this is a brand name for Dupont's elastane fiber. Can be machine washed and dried at a low heat.

Tencel Like Modal, Tencel is another type of rayon made from wood pulp, this one from the eucalyptus tree. Tencel is a brand name for this particular type of rayon, which is also known as lyocell. As with rayon, Tencel can be made to resemble silk, cotton, and linen and is often blended with these fibers. It is very absorbent with great drape. It is claimed that Tencel is the most sustainable of this regenerated group of fibers, as the eucalyptus trees from which it is made are grown sustainably. Best washed at lower temperatures.

Viscose Man-made but known as a regenerated fiber as it is made from wood pulp, viscose is a type of rayon, but made in a slightly different way. It has a beautiful heavy drape and is very

absorbent but slow to dry, which can make it uncomfortable to wear next to the skin. It's also prone to creasing. It is best washed at lower temperatures.

Wool A natural fiber from the fleece of animals such as sheep, goats, and even rabbits (includes alpaca, angora, and mohair), making it naturally warm. Although it is not absorbent, moisture can pass through its structure making it comfortable to wear; it is naturally breathable. Prone to shrinking and pilling, both of which are natural processes for wool, it needs to be handled carefully. Some wool fabrics are machine washable; check the label. If not, hand wash with a specialist gentle detergent and minimum agitation. Don't tumble dry wool; it's best dried flat.

Common knitted fabrics & fabric terminology:

Bouclé Used to describe a type of yarn or fabric. A bouclé yarn has irregular loops around it, which creates a textured surface on the fabric.

Boiled wool This can be textured or quite flat and almost felted in appearance. A medium- to heavyweight stable knitted fabric without much stretch.

Brushed back sweatshirt See French terry.

Cut & sew knits Often called sweater knits, these are fabrics with more of a "knitwear" look and so appear more like a traditional piece of knitted fabric.

They can be available felted (with a high wool content), offering a nice thick, warm, stable fabric. They can be very stretchy across the width, can shed, and unravel when cut; edges need to be neatened.

Double knit A dense knitted fabric that has less stretch than most knitted fabrics, and because it looks the same on both sides of the fabric there isn't a noticeable right and wrong side. Ponte roma, interlock, and scuba can be described as double knit fabrics.

French terry Typically known as sweatshirt fabric, or loopback sweat. Can be medium- to heavy in weight,

the right side is flat and smooth and looks like a knitted fabric, the back has a texture made up of loops of threads (which can look like terry toweling). This construction makes it comfortable to wear as the cotton is absorbent, but the textured wrong side can trap heat. The loops on the wrong side can also be brushed (known as fleece back or brushed back sweat) making it soft against the skin. Hardwearing as it tends to be made from cotton or a polyester/cotton mix.

Interlock A double knitted fabric that looks the same on the right and wrong side. Usually in cotton, it is a bit heavier than single jersey and is soft

and comfortable to wear. Although one of the stretchier double knit fabrics, it doesn't have great stretch recovery as it tends not to contain spandex (elastane). Scuba is technically a type of interlock but made with man-made fibers including spandex.

Fleece Always made from man-made or regenerated fibers, this fabric starts out like French terry but is brushed on both sides instead of just one. This makes a soft fabric on the inside as well as the outside, which traps air (making it warm to wear) and improves its water-repellent quality.

Jersey The most basic and common knitted fabric, this looks like hand knitting (stockinette/stocking stitch) on a tiny scale. Most T-shirts are made from single jersey. Commonly available in cotton, viscose, bamboo, wool, or silk, and often combined with spandex.

Loopback sweat See French terry.

Marl or Melange A colour effect usually found in knitted fabrics in which two different colors appear blurred. The most recognizable example is gray marl sweatshirt fabric. It is made by combining different colors of fibers plied or twisted together to create a single multicolored yarn, which is then used to construct the fabric.

Pilling The bobbling that occurs on the surface of some knitted fabrics through wear. Some wool does this naturally and the pills can be shaved off easily. When it occurs on man-made fiber fabrics it's difficult to remove and will keep recurring.

Ponte roma Sometimes called ponte di roma or just ponti or ponte, or roma! Ponte di roma means "Roman Bridge," which describes the texture on the surface of the fabric. Another type of double knit/interlock fabric, it is usually quite thick and heavy and so can be used for more structured dresses and jackets. Often made from a man-made fiber, such as a mix of polyester and viscose, and can also contain spandex. The best quality ponte roma is just viscose and spandex and this type is far less likely to pill than man-made polyester ponte. Rarely you can get cotton-rich ponte roma, which is great quality fabric as it washes well and won't pill.

Rib/ribbing Rib fabric has distinctive vertical ridges running along the length of the fabric formed by a regular pattern of knit and purl stitches. Often used as cuffs and neckbands on sweatshirts as it is very stretchy. It is usually cotton, polyester, wool, or acrylic.

Scuba A double knit, fairly dense fabric, usually in polyester and spandex made from fine fibers that give a very smooth surface. Scuba has a lot of stretch both vertically and horizontally. The high stretch, coupled with the slightly thicker weight and the fact it looks the same on both sides, makes it a very versatile fabric. Scuba is technically a type of interlock.

Single jersey See Jersey.

Sweater knits See cut & sew knits.

Sweatshirt See French terry.

4-way stretch/superstretch A performance knit fabric, usually single jersey or interlock in structure with a high spandex content allowing the fabric to have a high degree of stretch along the length as well as across the width, making it suitable for sports/performance clothing. It's also good for very fitted garments like leggings, as the lengthwise stretch means you won't get baggy knees! Usually polyester with spandex content of 10–20 percent. Often has a shiny surface due to the high synthetic content.

Washed wool See boiled wool.

SUPPLIERS

Here is a list of where you can source
good quality knitted fabrics:

US

The Fabric Store
www.thefabricstoreusa.com

Girl Charlee
www.girlcharlee.com

Hobby Lobby
www.hobbylobby.com

Joann Fabric & Craft Stores
www.joann.com

Michaels
www.michaels.com

Mood Fabrics
www.moodfabrics.com

UK

Discovery Knitting
www.discoveryknitting.co.uk

Ditto Fabrics
www.dittofabrics.co.uk

Faberwood
www.faberwood.com

Fabworks
www.fabworks.co.uk

Hobbycraft
www.hobbycraft.co.uk

John Lewis
www.johnlewis.co.uk

Minerva Crafts
www.minervacrafts.com

For more information on Wendy Ward:

Website/blog
wendyward.wordpress.com

Sewing classes and patterns
miyworkshop.co.uk

Instagram, Twitter, and Pinterest
@thatwendyward

Youtube
search: Wendy Ward

INDEX

Producing a book is a team effort and again it's been a joy to work with such a professional group of people who are all on my wavelength and "get" my vision.

A huge thanks to the fantastic team at CICO Books, especially Cindy Richards for backing me for a second time and commissioning the book I've been wanting to write since 2013! Anna Galkina has been a constant support; with encouraging words, expert ironing, and a great cup of tea, thank you Anna. Katie Hardwicke is the most thorough and speedy of editors and the styling by Rob Merrett and Nel Haynes (who stepped in at the last minute, thank you Nel), magically translated my vision into reality. Thank you also to Geoff Borin for the design of the book.

Once more, Julian Ward has transformed photographs of clothes into beautiful works of art; your eye for a great shot and perfect lighting is amazing Julian, thank you.

Of course, nothing is possible without supportive family and friends and someone who "has your back" at home. Big thanks and big love to Patrick and to my mum and dad, whom I'm sure still remain a bit mystified by what I spend my days doing but manage to say all the right things nevertheless.

I worked with some beautiful fabrics in this book which were generously provided by Discovery Knitting Ltd and Minerva Crafts. I am passionate about fair and local production and was proud to use Discovery's fabrics as they are all manufactured in Leicester, right here in the UK.

I also recently started to experiment with painting and printing my own fabrics, so was beyond excited to be able to use some in the Peak T-shirt, the Winnats Tank, and the Longshaw Skirt.

PATTERN SHEET KEYS

KEY TO SIZES (Bust / Waist / Hip)

— — — — — — — 31½ in. (80 cm) / 25¼ in. (64 cm) / 34¾ in. (88 cm)

••••••••••••••••••• 33 in. (84 cm) / 26¾ in. (68 cm) / 36¼ in. (92 cm)

—— —— —— 34¾ in (88 cm) / 28¼ in. (72 cm) / 38 in. (96 cm)

××××××××××× 36¼ in. (92 cm) / 30 in. (76 cm) / 39½ in. (100 cm)

———————— 38 in. (96 cm) / 31½ in. (80 cm) / 41 in. (104 cm)

- - - - - - - - - · 39¾ in. (101 cm) / 33½ in. (85 cm) / 43 in. (109 cm)

— - — - — - — - · 41¾ in. (106 cm) / 35½ in. (90 cm) / 45 in. (114 cm)

···················· 43¾ in (111 cm) / 37½ in. (95 cm) / 47 in. (119 cm)

××××××××××× 45¾ in. (116 cm) / 39¼ in. (100 cm) / 49 in. (124 cm)

· · · · · · · · · · · · 47¾ in. (121 cm) / 41½ in. (105 cm) / 51 in. (129 cm)

KEY TO PATTERNS

———————— Derwent Trousers

———————— Winnats Tank

———————— Monsal Lounge Pants

———————— Peak T-Shirt

———————— Kinder Cardigan

———————— Longshaw Skirt